HEAR OUR S

Hear our Silence

a journey into Prayer

John Skinner

"The Water that I shall give
will become a living spring within you
welling up to bring eternal Life"

Jn 4:14

Hear our Silence
People at Prayer

GRACEWING

First published in 1995 by HarperCollins

This edition published in 2003 by

Gracewing
2 Southern Avenue
Leominster
Herefordshire HR6 0QF

Cover photograph of a Carthusian monk at Parkminster by Graham Harrison. Reproduced by courtesy of *Saga Magazine*.

ISBN 0 85244 612 8

Printed in England by
Antony Rowe Ltd
Eastbourne BN23 6QT

To Dom Cyril
and the community of Parkminster

Et anima mea ipsi vivet,
semen meum serviet ei.
Psalm 22

CONTENTS

A First Encounter

I saw you under the fig tree.
John 1:50

THE Charterhouse at Parkminster in Sussex, six miles north of Devil's Dyke as the crow flies, is not difficult to find; it is merely that when you ask the way no one believes you wish to go there. They direct you repeatedly to the farm of the same name. And when you insist it is not the farmer but the monks you seek, there comes an involuntary two paces backwards – as if to say, 'You can't be serious!' They have a point: Parkminster is the home of the English Carthusians, the toughest monastic order in Christendom.

I had an appointment to meet the Prior at two o'clock on the hottest April day in fifty years. I wanted to discuss the possibility of my joining the community for a limited period to become familiar enough with their way of life to write a book. Yet above all, Carthusians are silent: they shy away from all publicity. I knew I had a tough task ahead of me.

Just ten to two. I at last located the sign saying ST HUGH'S CHARTERHOUSE and pulled into a winding, pot-holed drive leading to the priory. I found it clad in scaffolding. Three or four cars were parked in front. A workman clattered noisily about his business in the sky. Already I was preoccupied with the necessary silence of the place. I found it faintly shocking that its roof repairs should cause disturbance. Drawing a few deep breaths after my long haul from Somerset to Sussex, I crossed to the front door. Suddenly I was apprehensive at this first encounter with a Carthusian. What did I expect of the Prior?

First I had written; then we had spoken by telephone. I liked at once his soft Irish lilt, but already his tone displayed notable caution that I might join their life without being a *bona fide* candidate for admission to the Order. It was going to be difficult to persude him that there was anything in it for him. The Carthusians are by tradition utterly media shy.

I pulled the bell-rod beside the double oak doors. A loud chime bellied about within. I at once felt foolish; for now I spotted a telephone housed in a wooden box upon the wall with details of how to operate it and gain admission. An unexpected taste of the twentieth century. Fetching it down, I was surprised to be answered promptly. I was asked to wait; and presently a laybrother in a blue apron came to the grilled-squint set in the door. He smiled briefly, opened just a part of the great door and welcomed me inside.

'The Prior is expecting you?' he questioned.

My answer being satisfactory, he began to lead me into the interior. He had gone but two paces before he performed a deep bow from his waist, this directed outwards across the grassy courtyard. I realized his reverence was aimed in the direction of the church. Whether this was general custom or some private piety, I could not guess. But the message was clearly stated: you have come to the house of God.

We set out along an immense and anonymous cloister. We walked apart. I looked ahead, alert for any signal that we might be about to take a turning.

Presently, he startled me with the mundane remark, 'It's a lovely day!'

I murmured my agreement, and then found myself stranded in a dilemma: was this breaking of silence a courtesy to be taken up, or should I rather respect his own habitual silence and hold my peace . . .? I dithered, and the moment passed. Our pilgrimage continued.

We came at length, and I know not how, to a large hall. On its walls were great panels bearing heraldic shields which I could not at a glance interpret. He smiled, as if to tell me we

2

had arrived safely, and knocked at a partly open door. There was a muffled response from within, and I understood that I should go through.

The Prior had all the appearances of a yeoman farmer, even a rustic bee-keeper, far from the mien of Superior of the world's most illustrious enclosed Order of monks. His face was weather beaten, his cheeks rubicund, his nose had taken a thousand blows from the sun. He was five foot eight, wiry and alert. We shook hands, a good firm grasp: eye contact and ready smile along with it.

I was invited to sit down in a wooden armchair before his desk. He had been working outside, he explained, and would just go in and wash. I was left to contemplate the austerity of his office.

It was a large chamber, predominantly wood. An uncovered wooden floor, wooden chairs, the modest desk ahead of me made of pitch pine, its honey tone praised by the afternoon sunlight; and behind the desk a run of bookshelves, the length and height of the wall. I tried to decipher what books stood ranged there but found them hard to identify. To my left a large window through which the sun poured. A pleasing room for all its plainness.

Presently, Dom Cyril returned all smiles and apologies: he had forgotten, he admitted, I was coming. He laughed at his own failure, checked his diary upon the desk and, glancing at his steel wrist watch, praised my timekeeping.

I found him an easy man to meet. And began by telling him a little about myself, where I came from, what I had done in my life. My wife and family. He was a good and encouraging listener.

I knew well enough, I assured him, it was asking a great deal; my request to come and live with them lay somewhere on the table between us. But did he not feel, I pleaded, some need for the community's silent voice to be heard in today's world? He admitted that the Order was known only to a tiny section of people, even within the Catholic Church. Yet he repeated it was rare for outsiders to enter the monastery and share the daily routine of the monks except to try their vocation in the Order. He cited Charles de Foucauld (founder of an order of hermits in the Sahara). Irrelevant, I thought – that was France and a very long time ago. More recently (he appeared to sense my inner dissent) there had been a man who wanted to return to Vietnam to live a solitary life; he had stayed for six months at Parkminster, before fulfilling his ambition. Dom Cyril thought they had been able to help him . . . a little.

I opted for broadening the exchange to win time. I asked him about the repairs. The cost of upkeep, he admitted, was horrendous. The monastery was vast, built double-size half-way through the last century to accommodate at least two Carthusian communities – of the eight or so in France at that time – who were living under almost certain threat of expulsion. The axe had fallen, but as matters turned out they had stayed barely thirty years, leaving behind the nucleus of an emergent English community rattling around cloisters and accommodation designed to house four times their number. This disadvantage of sheer scale dogs them to this day.

We came back to the problem in hand. He startled yet encouraged me with mention of a persistent young TV producer who was also knocking at his door. His concept was to film the monks' day without any commentary. I was unclear whether this was to be literally a return to the silent movies or merely a skilful mode of breaking and entering; but I seized the opportunity to mount my decisive attack.

'Television is such a shallow medium!' I Muggeridged. 'I am convinced what you deserve is an old-fashioned, hand-held book. It might be very powerful.'

After this sally, I relaxed; I was never going to force the issue. But I sensed that things were beginning to flow my way.

He ruled out my living in proper cell quarters alongside the monks. 'That would get me the chop,' he chortled, then added, 'You could of course read all this up in a book,' mentioning Robin Bruce Lockhart's *Halfway to Heaven*, a work of unending sweetness and devotion.

'But I want to experience it from the inside,' I insisted. And in that moment, I knew we had a deal.

4

It was to be a compromise: I would be quartered in the guesthouse. It would be empty, he assured me, for most of my stay. From there I could follow the full daily and nightly routine of the community in as discreet and faithful a manner as possible. He rose from his desk at this conclusion and invited me to tour the monastery with him.

We returned to the hall outside, where a large painting shows a bird's-eye view of Parkminster. Together we now examined it closely.

The monks' quarters resemble a row of small detached houses, each with their own secluded, walled garden and joined at the front by the world's largest cloister. Some thirty in number, they are built around three sides of its square; at the centre is a five-acre orchard. Today, only a handful of these hermitages are lived in by choir monks. Across the top of the square, the cloister is completed by the complex of main community buildings – the church and chapter house, refectory and library.

We visited each in turn. Passing through large double doors beneath the 200-foot church spire, we were immediately in the graveyard: beyond lay a large orchard already in bud. It is a peaceful plot separated by low walls from the quiet orchard beyond. There are exactly ninety graves, banked like ancient tumuli. Each is crowned with a simple, stout wooden cross that bears no name or date. Only the weathering of the older crosses – now a dark and lichened brown – distinguishes them from more recent resting sites with their bright varnished wood. Here lies the harvest of 100 years of silence and prayer.

For a moment we stood together and joined their silence.

*

In the weeks leading up to my encounter with the Carthusians, I was inevitably playing a guessing game. What would it be like diving into the deep to behave like a monk of the thirteenth century? Would I stay the course more than five minutes? 'You'll be screaming after three days,' Dom Cyril had warned. How would I cope with three hours of prayer at midnight, the interminable drone of the Office with which I was utterly unfamiliar? What of the food regime? One large vegetarian meal each day at noon, then only a modest supper served at five in the evening. How would I fill my day completely on my own? Would the day-long silence deafen me?

I began to get into training. Four weeks to the day of my departure, I gave up booze. I would knock these worldly props away one by one, I told myself, feeling heroic. Then come the day, I would be fine, as sleek as a greyhound in the trap.

It was important too that I prepared my brief. I wondered what questions other people might have about this curious religious relic from the past not ten miles from Brighton beach. I began deliberately to drop word of it. 'I'm planning a book (pause) – about the Carthusians . . .' As a party piece, it frequently failed: few had even heard of them. But once they had been introduced as the SAS of the Christian Church, my audience were curious to learn more. Young people were specially intrigued by their challenge to the world, their statement of negation. Yet the questions and reactions of others could only prove a partial help: the quest was really my own.

The truth is, I had joined the Jesuits as I left school, aged nineteen, only to come away thirteen years later. My own unfinished business with God still haunted my journey forty years on. Shortly before going to Parkminster I had dreamed that I was editing a life of St Ignatius. It was not so much an editing exercise as an attempt to solve *The Times* crossword. Each sentence had to be twisted to a new shape and meaning, and there was only one suitable answer. The task seemed to take me all night long. It jogged a memory of my mother suddenly judging a piece of her knitting not to her liking and wiping it from her needles in order to start from scratch again, using the same wool but working a fresh pattern.

'Give me the boy at seven,' Ignatius is supposed to have said (in truth it was Pascal) 'and I will show you the man.' Ignatius had had me from nine to thirty-one, and he was still lingering on in my dreams: perhaps it was time to seek some answers.

*

What draws the Carthusian novice to Parkminster today? Father Cyril had spoken of his experience in France as a novice master handling the complex needs of today's young men, especially those coming off the Hippy Trail. 'The trouble is, what to say when someone tells you he is seeking God? You have to take him for real.' His task as novice master in England is rendered all the more difficult by the international intake of Parkminster. As the 'English-speaking Charterhouse', St Hugh's gathers in a widely varied trickle of God-seekers – men who have glimpsed a star (quite often in the East) and come back home to search its meaning.

Yet it is one thing to join the Hippy Trail in youthful search of global truth, cheap lifestyle and sublimating spiritual buzz, quite another to sign on with a bunch of Roman Catholic hermits whose unbroken tradition goes back 900 years to St Bruno. How can these two aspiring groups tie in and hope to find peace together under the self-same roof?

Consider what a young man is asked to give up when he becomes a monk. Any Roman Catholic religious at the successful conclusion of his noviceship will take the three vows of religion: poverty, chastity and obedience. Just as I had done in 1955 at the age of twenty: I had turned my back on women, on money, on having my own say in life – for good. Added to these three punitive, lifelong vows, the Carthusian makes two further promises – of stability and conversion. Yet by themselves alone, these three solemn promises cut to the quick a man's self-esteem, apparently removing all his first instincts and ambition. 'No wealth, no sex, no choice: for the remainder of my lifetime.' The religious is invited to set aside under these three heads all that keeps him from God. And with his vow of obedience and chastity, he literally gives himself heart, soul and body to his hero Christ.

Yet there is more to come for those who enter Parkminster to follow the Carthusian way. The Carthusian monk has joined the one monastery from where he will never move. Here he will expect to die in forty, fifty or sixty years. Again, he is to be a hermit. Not only has he forsaken women for good, but he has now embraced his own inner companionship, albeit within a community of like-minded hermits. His every day is spent alone. This day, and the next; and the one following. Alone as your own best and worst companion, making each day work from your own resources, borne along by the rhythmic regime that the Order has devised from centuries gone by.

Silence is golden. This silence is to last forever. No outside stimulae that good men may legitimately seek to enrich their minds and expand their souls: no music; only a few books, and these solely spiritual; no companionship other than the accidental community that this monastery happens to provide; no scholarship; no self-expression; no visual arts save that of nature as seen through a cloister grill. No aesthetics for the mind's tastes or comfort for the body – his food and drink of peasant style, his bed a straw palliase.

These are just some of the negative aspects of life that strike the outside observer. In so far as they impinge upon the real experience of our novice, they must be equally negative and in his experience yet more numerous and hard to bear. But as Aquinas might say, no one can act for a negative reason.

So why is he here? Let us ask him before we meet. He answers:

'I am looking for God. And in order to begin that quest, I start with myself. I must know myself, and then I may begin to know God.'

'It's a question of rhythm,' Dom Cyril murmurs.

And I hear Eliot intoning:

If you came this way,
Taking any route, starting from anywhere,
At any time or at any season,
It would be the same: you would have to put off
Sense and notion.

I

The Call to the Desert

Jesus began to talk to the people about John: 'What did
you go out into the wilderness to see? A reed swaying
in the breeze? No? Then what did you go out to see? A
man wearing fine clothes? Oh no, those who wear fine
clothes are to be found in palaces. Then what did you
go out for? To see a prophet? Yes, I tell you, and much
more than a prophet: he is the one of whom scripture
says: "Look, I am going to send my messenger before
you; he will prepare your way before you." '
Matthew 11:7–10

I drove out from Somerset at six in the morning. It was a day
of bright promise: I was eager to plunge headlong into it like a
warm shower. I came over Salisbury Plain, nodding to those
ancient stones now preserved in aspic by the smothering care
of English Heritage. Once long ago, coming in the other
direction in an ancient Ford station wagon at an equally early
hour, I had stopped the car. Stonehenge was mine alone.
Caressing those great stones one by one, I felt them to be holy
forerunners of Henry Moore. I enjoyed their weighty bounty,
drank in all they had to tell me from the mute substance of
their past. Now they stood strangely silent by the wayside as if
their tongues had been forever silenced; I felt no call to stop
today.

Traffic was light and I made good time. I had planned to
arrive by 10 a.m., since I had been warned that Monday was
the community walk day.

As I came to Parkminster, I thought of all those who had
come in the past, hoping never to leave. A brother, in dark-
blue overalls, was emerging from a doorway surrounded by

scaffolding which encased the front of the house like a steel vine. (It was my first encounter with Brother Augustine, the Dutchman, laundryman, engineer and maker of cider.) He struck me as somewhat severe as I asked him where to dispose of my car. He guided me into an inner courtyard and I drove through large steel-clad green doors. He secured the gates behind me, and I sat for a moment in the silence of my arrival. I was led away by Brother Richard, the same Brother door-keeper – he of the profound bow – whom I had met on my first visit. Passing through the grandiose outer hall with its escutcheons of the twelve British Charterhouses past, we reached the Prior's cell.

Cyril, as I now thought of him, greeted me warmly with his familiar smile and handshake. I felt a curious kind of home-coming. He greeted me as a friend and familiar. All hint of misgivings about my book had vanished: together we set out for the guesthouse which I knew to be set apart from the monastery.

We soon left the cloister and, passing through double glass doors, entered a grandly faded house, as if the monks had neglected it on purpose to punish its former flamboyant worldliness. The guest house is joined to the monastery buildings in two places – at its front and side – by cloisters, yet still contrives to stand apart. During the six years that Parkminster was building, the entire community lived here; at one time, they were eighteen in number, almost as many as live in the whole of the monastery today. They must have found it peculiarly confined, even though they spread into every part, from cellar rooms where they prayed to attics where they had their refectory. Today, it is furnished to accommodate perhaps half a dozen guests, but never is there such a houseful. I was told that I would be alone in this great echoing space with its institutional air, its ancient brown linoleum, numerous holy pictures and a plethora of saints standing stiffly on their plinths like watchmen on the walls of some city. These were the positive signs of religious dedica-tion. On the debit side, I felt at once the absence of a woman's hand: there were no soft furnishings, no attempt at a colour scheme; this was an all-male house with no concessions to comfort or the subtle art of home-making.

We climbed a back staircase; a gaudily coloured imitation of a della Robbia madonna greeted us on a half-landing before we came to a large study bedroom. 'Room number three' the Prior spelt out, as if I would be wise to memorize this address without delay. I blurted out that I would remember it by the Trinity, and then wished I had said nothing of the kind. It was a generous-sized room with large sash windows facing east and south. The monastery was gathering me in. This was to be my room for the duration of my stay, the cell I was to 'keep' to and follow a routine in imitation of the seclusion of a choir monk. I laid my case to one side and, sitting facing the Prior before a large desk, began to learn more about the monastery's daily life.

My monk's kit had been prepared for me: an alarm clock to wake me at midnight and again at dawn and a handful of books. On the large, office-style desk with its numerous cubby-holes and little drawers were a Latin/English psalter, a Latin Gem dictionary and, lying separate atop of an ancient, chaise-style *prie-dieu* in the far corner of the room, an attractive calf-bound book. This was the Carthusian Day Offices in English recited by each monk in cell. Lastly, I was handed a printed sheet setting out the daily timetable. Father Cyril has a wonderfully calming manner: 'Just let it flow around you. Drop all thoughts and worries from outside.' He went through the day's programme in detail. I was to join the community for the two Offices said publicly in church, the Night Office of Matins and Lauds and each afternoon at 3.45 for Vespers, praying with them in the choir stalls, and also joining them at their daily community Mass at eight in the morning. For the remainder of the day, just like the choir monks in their hermitages, I too would keep to my own cell and attempt to follow the day's routine of prayer, reading and spiritual exercises. Apart, that is, from a stint in the kitchen at one in the afternoon.

'It's really quite simple,' lilted the Prior, his soft Irish accent providing much-needed assurance. 'Let it flow over you,' he said again. 'It's just being a Christian, the presence of God and *Lectio Divina* . . .' He made it sound simple enough: I only hoped it would turn out to be that simple. I was willing to try, for even if in joining these professionals I fell well short of them, at least I might glimpse some reality of their prayer-filled days and nights. At least I would be right in the front line, not like the bevvy of foreign correspondents who file reports of 'gunfire at the airport' from the safety of their hotel bar.

*

We left the guesthouse to explore the monastery. I was shown how to find the church and where the kitchen lay across the cobbled yard below. Then it was back to the confines of my room. The Prior left me with the promise that he would come and see me in two or three days 'to see how you are getting on'. I saw him to the door and closed it after him: my solitude had begun.

I sat down at the ancient desk to study the timetable:

Spiritual Exercises	11.50	Rise.	
	12.00	Matins B.V.M.	
	12.30	Matins & Lauds in Church.	
		In cell: Lauds B.V.M.	*(3½ hours)*
Rest	3.30–6.50	Sleep.	*(3 hours)*
Spiritual Exercises	6.50	Rise.	
	7.00	Primes/Terces.	
	8.00	Conventual Mass in Church.	
		In cell: Thanksgiving, Spiritual Reading.	*(3½ hours)*
Study/Work/Meal	10.30	Manual work.	
	11.15	Sexts.	
	11.45	Dinner. Recreation or Light Work.	
	1.15	Angelus. Nones.	
	1.30	Study.	
	3.00	Manual Work.	*(5 hours)*

Spiritual Exercises	3.30	Vespers B.V.M.	
	3.45	Vespers in Church.	
		In cell: Spiritual Exercises.	
		Supper.	
	6.15	Mental Prayer. Examen.	
	6.45	Complines.	
		Private Devotions.	
	7.45	Retire.	*(4 hours)*
Rest	7.45–11.50	Sleep.	*(4 hours)*

I looked again at this daunting daily programme which I was to attempt. It felt so austere that I could only speculate upon the human experience of living such an ascetic routine, knowing that it would be repeated exactly the same tomorrow and the next day and the next until life's end. Bossuet, the great French preacher, spoke in praise of monastic life as a daily repetitive cycle without seam: 'Each day like the last, year on year until death . . .' He intended to eulogize yet ended by making it sound as attractive as a loveless marriage. As an academic friend commented of the Carthusian life: 'They must have something going for them or no one would stay around.'

A quick computation which I annotated on the timetable revealed that a monk spends eleven hours of his day in prayer and spiritual exercises, five hours either working, studying or eating and the remainder asleep in two periods (of four hours and three) separated by the Night Office. Austere in the extreme, but in one respect was it not somehow familiar? And then I recognized the attributes of the school timetable: the day broken down deliberately into manageable periods, none longer than three-quarters of an hour, like stepping-stones across a river wherein otherwise we flounder. Perhaps the knack is a combination of living in the present while conjuring the eternal: Blondin crossed Niagara – one foot before the other, never looking down until he reaches the other side.

I was brought to my senses by a knock at my door. It was

already 11.45: Bede, the pantryman, had arrived with my lunch box. He asked kindly if I knew my way to the church; did I know where to sit for the Offices? I reassured him, hoping I was right, and that I would know where to go at the appointed time. Then I carried the mysteriously weighty contraption he had delivered across to my table, spread the small cloth provided and laid my solitary setting before the open window. The lunch box measured two feet square by some ten inches deep and bore my room's identity – Number 3 – upon its side. It had a stout wooden carrying handle, and its front was a shutter sliding upwards to reveal its varied contents.

First to hand, a nest of stainless steel food containers stacked three high: today's hot food. The saucepan-like containers are known as gamelles, the French word for dixy such as soldiers or scouts of old would have used in the field, a legacy of La Grande Chartreuse, the mother house in France. Monks eat directly from these saucepans: plates are considered a luxury.

Today there is onion soup in the lowest gamelle followed by three eggs on soggy white toast in the next and finally a generous helping of mashed potatoes and carrots in the uppermost. I explore further and find a Grolsch beer bottle filled with an excellent home-produced cider wine. A quarter of a large brown loaf lies neatly in a plastic bag and, upon an upper shelf, several much-used plastic containers, their washed-out logos of forgotten margarine brands hiding new surprises. Here I find fresh fruit aplenty – five apples and an orange – cheese, Flora spread and a surprise helping of peanuts. As an aside, a small dish of excellent honey with a final frivolity, a common-and-garden packet of crisps. As I slowly do justice to this thoughtfully balanced food supply, I begin to think about the monks. Already they seem less mysterious as I picture them also exploring and digesting an exactly similar lunch.

*

On my first visit to Parkminster, the Prior had taken me into an empty hermitage to show me its accommodation. I expressed surprise at the generous space; it was the size of a comfortable two-up, two-down cottage. 'But a monk needs space,' he countered, doing a shadow boxing mime. I took his point: a hermit would have countless inner tensions which he must needs release. The Carthusian took on a new heroic role – the solitary athlete in continuous training for a super-human contest. I conjured visions of St Anthony and his hermit companions of the desert living long ago in Thebaide.

The hermitage door opens from the cloister; each is identi-fied by a letter of the alphabet and a name-plate which bears its own distinct tessera in Latin. These vary from pious to preachy. Thus cell HH reads *Bone JESU exaudi me intra tua vulnera absconde me*, a snippet from *Anima Christi*, the four-teenth-century eucharistic prayer to Christ ('Good Jesus, hear me: hide me within your wounds'). And two doors down, the ultimate saying of Christ which marks him out as Lord: *Qui perdiderit animam suam propter me, inveniet eam, dicit DOM* ('Whoever loses his soul on my account will find it, says the Lord'). But my own favourite is the enigmatic *Ad quid venisti?* ('To what have you come?'). On the left of each door is a hatch, where every day at 11.30 lunch is delivered. Hanging from the door-frame is a rope bell-pull which rings upstairs in the monk's bedroom to signal a visitor, that rare and barely welcome event. Not even the Prior may enter a monk's cell without his permission, but if a visitor is expected, the accepted custom is that he lifts the latch with his *passe-partout* and enters in. The hermitage is each one's own sacred terri-tory, the ground of his solitude. And when a monk enters another's cell, the door is always left open (according to the Rule) until the caller leaves. Such visits are not encouraged and only take place if there is real business to conduct. A priest might be asked to hear another's confession, a novice may give an English lesson to a fellow monk from a distant land or some house duty must be settled. Otherwise, for less important and non-urgent business, a note is left in the hatch or on the doorstep.

The first space inside a hermitage is the *ambulacrum*, a passageway of some twenty yards running the full length of the house where a monk may pace his thoughts or recite his rosary. At right angles and running the width of the hermitage on the ground floor are two chambers some fifteen feet by eighteen: the first, without door and opening to the garden, is a fuel store where coal and wood lie heaped. Logs are delivered large and unsplit. Chopping up his log supply provides a monk with continual exercise throughout the winter. The second room, his workshop, may contain a wood-turning lathe or workshop bench together with appropriate tools. Formerly, items of furniture were traditionally made or repaired in cell. Indeed, the great architect of English monastic revival in the tenth century, St Dunstan, himself an accomplished silversmith, insisted that all his monks practise and perfect some kind of craftsman's skill. But at Parkminster today, little of this tradition remains, although some brothers still practise the art of book-binding.

In the centre of the hermitage lies a garden which is completely private, sheltered from its neighbour by high walls. Each monk is free to plant as he pleases, whether to produce vegetables or grow flowers and shrubs. As I would discover, every garden announces the identity of its incumbent to a marked degree. One is shaded and wildly overgrown with an abundance of shrubs and climbers on the wall, so that a regular family of fly catchers are reared within its privacy each year. Dom Bogdan would win prizes in the onion class at almost any village flower show, while the Dom Bruno's suspect heart rules out his digging any more, so that all he now has is a flourishing crop of weeds and thistledown.

Stairs lead up to the two living rooms on the first floor. The first chamber, measuring eighteen by fifteen feet, is known as the Ave Maria. It contains a prominent statue of Our Lady: each time a monk returns to his cell, he kneels to pray a Hail Mary. She who 'kept all these things in her heart' is the contemplative's champion; the Carthusian recites the Office of Our Lady throughout his day. Some monks furnish this room and use it for reading or typing, while others have it completely bare. Beyond is a second, slightly larger room, which serves as living-room cum study, bedroom and oratory.

Along the wall is a fitted wooden box-bed with plank sides not unlike a ship bunk, with a thick straw palliase and a single rough pillow. Beside the bed is a fitted oratory with *prie Dieu* and cupboards for prayer books and psalter. Over by the window is a small table with a mug, a glass and cutlery where the monk eats his two daily meals alone, looking out over his garden. In this empty hermitage I was shown by the Prior, the garden was silent and untended. At its centre the stump of what had once been a sizeable monkey puzzle tree; on the north wall a bird box lay empty, yet to attract any permanent residents this season.

As well as bedroom and oratory, this room is also the monk's study with desk and a modest shelf or two for books. If the monk is still studying for the priesthood there are his philosophical and next his theological courses to follow; once ordained, choir monks may pursue their own bent in study. However, Carthusians are not scholars; they never write for publication and the one or two works to appear from time to time always bear the anonymous attribution, 'by a Carthusian'.

Formerly, the hermitage was only heated by a primitive wood stove in the bedroom. Just recently, this has been replaced by a wood-and-coal-burning unit which provides hot water and a drying radiator on the landing outside. The sluice in the Victorian washplace has been replaced with a shower (hot water in winter, cold in summer), and there is a modern flushing loo.

I warmed to the idea of playing monk in one of the many empty hermitages and in all innocence asked the Prior if it would be possible. But the cell, like the Carthusian habit, is the sacred outer sign of his journey into solitude and his search for the presence of God. It is not given lightly to outsiders but is reserved for genuine candidates testing their Carthusian calling. Listen to the Master of Novices encouraging his young men to take their first hesitant steps:

> God needs nothing of our wealth. But he does need our poverty, through which, alone, we may receive his gifts, his love, himself. God is not able to be himself, to be love,

17

if he is not able to be self-outpouring into our hearts in
the extravagant folly of his gratuitous love.

Treasure therefore your thirst for the living God.

One of the most beautiful definitions of a monk is that
he is a man of desire. This restlessness does not allow
him to be content with what is created; the thirst for the
absolute, this hunger for love, is the wellspring, the
impetus for his search for God.

(The Way of Silent Love, *p. 28*)

This desire is born of a naïve love of God, the response, as it
were, to take God for real and seek to allow him to dominate
your life. The contemplative has first been touched by God.
He has fallen for him. Think of 'young love' familiar to us in
the world; two young people seen holding hands at a bus stop
or arm in arm as they walk along the street. Their bodies need
to touch, reassure, care, enwrap: at every step they seek this
bodily message of contact which tells their heart's involve-
ment. Oblivious to the outside world: if it impinges, they are
happy to shut it out. The same is true of the Carthusian. He
has chosen to shut himself away in his solitude, a solitude he
guards tenaciously, for his business is with God, and it will
keep him a lifetime.

*

I ate my first Carthusian meal before my open window,
admiring the fine June day. The food was plentiful and sensibly
varied, when I had expected nautical hard tack. There was even
an element of play, which I found quite comic, as if the kitchen
were intent on offering continual surprises to the hermit
palate. I was reminded of Iris Murdoch's *The Sea, the Sea*, where
we learn that solitary eating often leads the palate to grow
distorted – cold baked beans are praised with comic
eloquence. Bede, the prankster pantryman of Parkminster,
goes in for similar special surprises, presenting the taste buds
with continual challenge. Following a formidable triangle of
omelette one inch thick served with spinach and roast potatoes, try the sensation of prunes with fresh-picked raspberries;

or again, peanut-butter on cheese or marmalade spread thick upon a currant bun. Delights that still lay in the future: this present box of surprises would do for my first main meal at Parkminster; it was sustaining and more than sufficient. At the very least I would not starve.

II

The Carthusians of England

I am living in the wilderness of Calabria,
miles away from any other homes.
    St Bruno

T H E warm June sun invited me into the guesthouse garden
lying below my open window. Lapping L-shaped around the
house and enclosed by ten-foot-high walls, it was depress-
ingly overgrown with mature bay, holly and apple trees
crowding too near the house for comfort and, thirty yards into
the garden by the boundary, two sizeable horse chestnuts.
The grey walls pressed in like purposeful custodians, menac-
ingly topped out with a double sling of barbed wire through
which oblivious squirrels skipped. And against these walls
grew an impenetrable tangle of brambles, wild rose and ivy.
Underfoot lay rotting the rough-mown grass of early spring,
smothering all new growth. This the only sign of human care:
no serious gardener can have lingered here for fifty years. The
house too was flaky beyond belief. Its last coat of paint
decades since, yet somehow it looked modestly robust, a
distant tribute to the honesty of its builder. It appeared essen-
tially a bachelor house, builder-designed with, one suspects,
overmuch advice from its founder owner. An escutcheon
across the main door gave his initials only, yet adjacent
anchors seemed to hint of a sailor home from the sea.
Certainly, his architectural ideas had proved to be severely
practical rather than aesthetic. But in most of these early
guesses, I was to be proved quite wrong.

The original owner, William Percival Boxall, described as a

successful merchant, had built a stylish house to his own design and laid out the surrounding parkland ten miles inland from the Sussex coast in a quiet backwater. Contemporary photographs show a striking mansion, faced in local undressed downland flint and graced with many pleasing details – a noble belvedere rising above the main door boasts an elegant oriel window. The Carthusians later stripped the house to its bare bones and compounded this outrage by rendering the entire facade in battleship grey cement. The first book of the Parkminster Annals speciously explains that the original walls were somewhat thin and needed to be strengthened. Together with its farm, the land amounted to 110 acres. Squire Boxall – his territory also took in the ancient manor of Ewhurst – completed the house in 1869 but had lived there with his wife and daughter for less than five years before mounting debts forced him to seek a buyer. The Carthusians of La Grande Chartreuse had been eyeing England as one of several possible bolt-holes for their French communities, should the mounting tide of anticlericalism force them abroad. (They were proceeding with similar plans in Spain at the same time.) Their first thoughts turned to the county of Somerset, where the very first English house had been established in the twelfth century at Witham by Henry II as part of his penance for the death of Thomas Beckett. Accordingly, the local Bishop of Clifton was approached to see if a suitable property – an existing large house set in secluded acreage – could be located somewhere in Somerset. (Under Canon Law, the local Ordinary must license any new religious foundation.) But then the parish priest of West Grinstead, himself a Frenchman who had come to England in response to the Bishop of Southwark's appeal for priests, heard word of the possible sale of Parknowle in Sussex, whose present owner was experiencing certain cash-flow problems. It was possible that it might suit the monks' requirements.

Two Carthusian negotiators currently touring England were invited to West Grinstead to view. The Catholic camp was apprehensive that Squire Boxall, who was described as a 'zealous Protestant', would be disinclined to sell to Catholic priests, even less so to foreign monks. Accordingly, a sub-terfuge was arranged. Using the pretext of a neighbourly call and that polite interest which was only to be expected when a gentleman has recently established himself in style, the three priests contrived to be invited for tea at Parknowle so as to be shown around the entire estate incognito. The parish priest was known, but the two Carthusians wearing ordinary dress were simply introduced to Mr Boxall as 'friends on holiday'. Yet one of them, however, needed special mention: he was introduced as a former general in the Russian army, none other than the Baron Nicholaÿ.

More than satisfied with all they had seen, the two emissaries reported back to Father General and purchase procedures were put in train. Through the good offices of Messers Arnold, a Catholic solicitor's practice in London, Mr Boxall was advised that 'a certain Russian gentleman' who had recently visited Parknowle would now like to buy it. Contracts were signed and exchanged in Brighton on 21st January 1873.

The Annals admit without apology that the conspirators maintained their incognito even up to the exchange of con-tracts, when they 'were scrupulous to hide their Carthusian qualities'. But when Dom Jean-Louis de Nicolaÿ, dressed in a fur-lined cloak against an inclement English January, appended his signature with the address La Grande Chartreuse, he was closely questioned. 'You live in the vicinity, perhaps?'

'No, at La Grande Chartreuse . . .' he replied.

English humour came to the rescue, and it is said the two parted excellent friends. Mr Boxall could afford to be generous, since his money problems were at an end. He had achieved a toppy price, as the Carthusians were the first to admit. In all they had paid £18,000: £13,000 for the house (valued at a mere £7,000) and £45 per acre (whereas £40 was deemed a fair 'middle price'). Yet they had achieved their aim: a desert soli-tude ripe for development not ten miles from La Manche. It must have seemed a home from home – just over the water. Indeed, in the first volume of Annals (the house records are beautifully scripted with chapter initials embellished in the ancient manner) there is a charming, softly coloured map derived from Magna Carta. It shows Hamfeld (Henfield) more or less in the centre of the ancient Sussex of 1066 that was at that time heavily wooded across its northern boundary with Sudrie (Surrey), while Hantescire lies to the west and Chenth to the east. The main towns marked and named are Cicestre, Lewes, Penevesel (with Harundel Castle nearby) and, of course, Hastings, where the saga of the Conquest had begun. One can sense the artist-scribe of the Carthusians rejoicing in a recapitulation of that famous invasion of England's green and pleasant land. Now nine centuries later, the French are back, he seems to boast; and this time they come on God's commission.

*

Returning to my room, I sat down to read the life of St Hugh (yes, he of Lincoln with his pet swan), the founding father of the English Carthusians, the first Carthusian to be sainted. Adam of Eynsham, its author, was a Benedictine prior who was chaplain to Hugh in the last three years of the saint's life. When the 'turbulent priest' Archbishop Becket had been slaughtered at the indirect word of the king before his own high altar in Canterbury, Henry II repented and sought forgiveness from the Pope. He was told that for his penance he must spend three years on crusade in the Holy Land. He bargained instead to found three monasteries – Benedictine, Franciscan and Carthusian.

For the latter, a suitable parcel of unwanted king's land was identified at Witham in remote Somerset. It was poor land and much of it hunting forests, but this mattered little, for unlike the Cistercians, Carthusians have no ambition to be farmers. All they seek is solitude. A stream of funds were allocated – rents and revenues from farmlands and some few due from 'alien' priories, religious houses founded from France. The monks may have found it increasingly difficult to collect these dues as time passed; but at its very beginning, there is no doubting the king's best intentions to fund his new monastery at Witham generously so as to secure its permanent foundation. His thoughtful generosity even descended to such particulars as their wine supply. (Perhaps he had overlooked the fact that his monks were moving into countryside where the Normans had successfully established the cider apple from their native land.) Witham's cellars were to claim yearly four pipes of Gascon red wine, part of the king's own supplies landed in the port of London. Above all Henry's founding charter gave them a generous parcel of land over which they alone had complete jurisdiction. It all added up to demonstrate amply his desire to atone for Becket's death. Yet at the same time, he was doing no more than many in his position seized the chance to do: the founding benefactor of a monastery would, as it were, be taking out a heavenly permanent life policy. Generation after generation of monks would pray for the souls of their benefactors, so speeding them on their sure way to heaven.

In 1181, a small group of French monks arrived at the Forest of Selwood to establish this first charterhouse in England. At once they met with deep hostility from the locals. The king's dictats were fine on the parchment foundation deed, but their realization in practice meant a large group of working farmers and their families were about to be evicted from their tenancies. Moreover, the agents of this outrage were foreign monks, cowled and silent.

Country folk have their ways of resisting unwanted incomers, even those franchised by the king himself. The Somerset foundation so nearly failed on the stony soil of local hostility; after a period of struggle the first Prior returned to France in despair. But the king was not prepared to let slip his eternal salvation lightly. He took counsel about the Carthusians from an English knight who had lived in France. He was informed that one of the most respected and talented Carthusians in the whole of France was Hugh of Avalon: learned and courteous, here was a monk loved by all. This was to be his man. After some difficulties, the king at last had his way and Hugh arrived to become Prior at Witham. His first task was to settle the local people with justice; he persuaded the king to offer the tenant farmers generous alternative land, some as far away as Oxfordshire, so that every displaced family was properly resettled. This root difficulty overcome, Hugh set about establishing the charterhouse on a sound footing, planning its new building layout and soon attracting a steady flow of new recruits. In spite of an extensive building programme which soaked up much of its annual income, Witham was soon flourishing. Yet all this quiet success made Hugh a public man and, much against his will, he was created bishop of Lincoln, one of the largest bishoprics in England, whose spiritual and temporal territories lapped down as far as Oxfordshire.

The saint is always shown with a swan at his side. Shortly after the new bishop arrived to take charge of his diocese a male swan flew in and drove all rivals away. It also took a fancy to bishop Hugh, who reciprocated the bird's attentions. The myth goes that whenever the bishop was about to return from his travels, the bird would somehow know and on the day of his arrival would be present at the gate to greet him. In spite of his constant business as bishop, Hugh remained a Carthusian of Witham at heart, making regular visits to his monks until his death.

The Carthusian Order in England extended only slowly over the next 300 years. The contemplative is always far less numerous than the active vocation. However, when Henry VIII brutally suppressed them, putting eighteen of their number to death, there were eleven foundations throughout England, including two influential houses in London.

*

It was time to investigate the book of psalms lying on my desk, beginning with the introduction. I knew very little about them; Jesuits do not sing the office in choir, for they are an active Order. Only when ordained do they recite the Office in private, like any other priest. For my twenty-first birthday, I had received a present from my family of a Latin psalter which I had used from time to time without ever visiting much inner meaning or forming any great attraction for their metier. If I was to spend many hours praying them at last, it was high time to learn more about their meaning and importance.

The psalms form the major part of the Divine Office, the Opus Dei, or God's Work, which from earliest times has been the Church's official prayer spanning the whole day and forming one of the contemplative's chief tasks. While priests will simply find private time in their day to pray the Office alone, monks come together to sing and perform it liturgically. Its history is as ancient as the Church itself. The three day hours, Terce, Sext and None, derive from the practice in the very early Church of commemorating the 'hours' of Our Lord's last day, Christ's arrest, his crucifixion and finally, at the ninth hour, his death. Christians, and especially women, would gather together to sing psalms regularly through the day every third hour. This women-led prayer structure established a basic pattern to which was later added morning prayer or Matins and finally night prayers or Compline. Matins is either said at dawn or, in the case of some stricter religious orders, in the middle of the night. It is by far the longest of all the Offices, lasting some two hours, and on feast-days it is embellished by elaborate plainsong antiphons as well as additional readings and may last as long as three hours.

Nervous of navigating the cloistered maze, I set out in good time before the 3.45 bell sounded for Vespers. The layout of Parkminster is in reality quite straightforward: the church is centrally placed, the great cloister with the choir monks' hermitages lies in a square to the west, and above it a smaller quadrangle known as the garth or garden complements it on the eastern side of the church. But to the novice cloisters all look alike; moreover those at Parkminster appear to stretch away for ever.

As it was, I took only one wrong turn and arrived at church just as a monk began to toll the bell. At its bidding a steady file of monks soon wound their way to church from all over the monastery. It was my first sight of the monks *en masse* and I was intrigued by it. The Carthusian habit is white all over, consisting of a loose-fitting habit over which is worn the scapula, a long white apron which falls down almost to the hemline back and front. It is secured to the side by two slashes of material that tether front and back just below pocket height; they are amply cut and fall outwards from the top, so that seen from behind they resemble turned out pockets or side pouches. The cowl is always worn up over the head so that it flops well forward to lend a monk anonymity when he is walking abroad and afford him maximum custody of the eyes. Novice monks wear a black cloak over their white habit. Among the monks in the opposite stalls, I notice two laymen have appeared.

The community enters the church through double doors which bring them directly before the high altar. They then file down to take their places in the choir stalls. It is a fine, high-roofed building with a splendid acoustic; austere in the manner of the Carthusians, who permit neither organ nor much ornament in their worship. The walls are oak panelled throughout to a height of some twenty feet. The high altar is plain and somewhat forbidding; no longer used for Mass, its sole remaining function is the reservation of the Blessed Sacrament. It is plainly furnished with crucifix and altar cloths: only on major feasts are there flowers. In line with the liturgical reforms following the Vatican Council thirty years ago, Mass is now said on a simple table altar set in the centre of the church, the priest facing forward for all to see. The nave is lined with choir stalls which run down both sides. While across the lower end of the church facing the altar, the Prior sits in his presiding stall.

As each monk enters the church, he blesses himself with holy water and, advancing into the church a little way, offers a profound bow towards the high altar. (The genuflection towards the Blessed Sacrament common to Catholics is never used, suggesting it to be of more recent origin.) Then moving across to the bell rope which hangs from the ceiling directly before the altar, he takes his turn tolling perhaps no more than two or three pulls before handing it on as the next brother arrives. It is an endearing and meaningful expression of a community of hermits calling themselves together for common prayer.

On this occasion, my first attendance at public Office, I took none of this in. I understood the Prior to have told me to go to the right-hand stalls – 'right at the end'. Seeing a white figure standing utterly still and facing towards the altar, I stood in the stall directly ahead of him. But as soon as the Prior arrived, he shepherded me to a different stall where the body of monks stood in line together lower down the body of the church. (The lone monk was Brother Ignatius: I was to learn that some brothers joined in with the choir monks to sing the Office, while others preferred to maintain the old practice of listening to the Gregorian chant in silence and apart.) To compound my confusion, as soon as I had gained my new place, I managed to dislodge the misericord tip-up seat, which went down with a resounding crash. I had arrived.

Vespers is sung in English apart from the antiphons, which remain in Latin; the fifteen minutes of prayer end with the Magnificat, Mary's canticle, which Luke puts into her mouth as she greets her cousin Elizabeth with the news of her pregnancy. At its close, I limped back to the guesthouse to spend the final hours of the day as the timetable indicated. Spiritual reading; supper of sardines on toast and a salad; mental prayer, examination of conscience. Compline and into bed by eight o'clock, while it was still light. I had much to think about, but I slept soundly – for four hours.

*

When first we met, the Prior had referred to the special quality of the night prayer, but no one could have prepared me for the amazing explosion of energy, the simple, tugging drama of that first night of Matins.

Although I had carefully packed a torch for my stay, I foolishly left this behind in my room and chose to grope my path downstairs by moonlight as the 12.30 bell tolled. I was naïvely confident of finding my path to the church without difficulty. I managed to escape the echoing dark of the guesthouse and came into the cloisters without mishap, listening all the while to the great bell tolling its summons. At once the cloisters by night seemed anonymous, their dark confusion inviting in every direction. I came to the wooden partition door leading into the main cloister; I had no need of my *passe-partout* that I was clutching, for it was already open. And now one or two shadowy figures were moving at right angles to me in the middle distance. And then, mercy, with a sudden dart in my direction a white-clad figure invited me to follow him. I was saved but even so, he set out at such a pace that I could barely see him ahead. As my eyes adjusted to the habit of my saving guide, I reflected that perhaps Carthusians wore white for this very purpose: just as deer have white butts to take safe flight through darkening thickets. Presently, we turned the corner and an electric light clicked on. Now one could see the purposeful file of white- and black-clad monks, cowls over their heads, converging on the church.

After my hopeless entry at Vespers, I thought I would wait a while until the main body of monks had gone ahead. I stood against the wall opposite the church doors and watched the monks file in. Almost at once, a choir monk came across to me and announced: 'Now don't stand around there in the cold: come along inside.' Without further ceremony, he took me into my stall and made sure I was settled. This was Dom Bruno, the Father Vicar (deputy Prior).

The special giant-sized night psalters and antiphona used at Matins sit propped upon wooden book-rests. Leather-bound and studded against fifty years' use, they contain the complete annual cycle of Matins and Lauds throughout the liturgical year. Two monks share a single psalter, moving deftly from one passage to the next, their places guarded by brightly coloured ribbons. Once the books have been opened and places marked, each monk faces towards the altar in silent prayer. A taper is lit from the sanctuary lamp to light a second lamp in the centre of the choir suspended from the ceiling high above. The purpose of this second lamp is purely functional: before the church enjoyed electricity, it was lit by means of oil lamps at every stall. When reading from the Lectern, a monk would have to swing down this great lamp and ignite a taper in order to light the lamp on the Lectern.

As the last monk arrives, the bell-ringer replaces the bell

29

rope on its hook beside the great church door and, with everyone in his place, all lights are extinguished.

The community gathers its spiritual energy in silence; an intense moment of concentration falls like a deep slumber upon the assembly. I am aware that the business skills of this group of monks are solely to pray; I am carried in their silence that reaches out to God.

The church is utterly still: dark, save only for the dim red glow of the two lamps. I gaze up into the black void of the church ceiling, where high above a dim flicker answers the two lamps below. The monks turn inwards for a moment of sustained silence, the prayer in preparation for the long Office about to sound out. It is a fulcrum in time between one day's prayer, which has just been concluded, and the next day, opening out its fresh undulating rhythm of prayer, liturgy and work in the presence of God.

There comes a humble human yawn as a monk succumbs to natural tiredness. Then the intense silence floods back as this rare group of prayermen focus their souls in loving atten-tion upon their God, asking for his presence, opening their hearts to his promised Spirit.

The Prior makes three knocks with his key upon the pew. And there is a shuffle as the two groups rise to face the altar once more. The signing with the symbol of Christ's cross. And softly, almost hesitantly, comes the Prior's invitation to prayer: *'Domine, labia mea aperies: Et os meum annunciabit laudem tuum'* ('Lord, open my lips: and my mouth will declare your praise').

Then follows the Gloria Patri, the doxology of thanksgiving to the Trinity. It is sung, as it were, in slow motion, prayerfully and with great reverence, as each monk, perched upon his misericord, bows low. Then comes a precisely measured, utterly silent pause that breaks the trinitarian doxology before the concluding phrase is joined: *'Sicut erat in principio et nunc et semper et in saecula saeculorum. Amen.'* Its power concentrates the holy meaning of the prayer. The familiar words, exuded so reverently in this strange, slow chant, pierce some kind of supernatural barrier as if man's time has been transcended to glimpse God's own arching non-time reaching across the whole span of his Creation, from its very inception to its invisible ending: the rainbow arc.

Words are live: 'Glory to Father, Son, Holy Spirit: as it was from the start, is at this moment and will be for all time – and beyond.'

*

Every second stall has a rocker-switch concealed beneath its arm and these are now flicked on. The choir stalls suddenly come to life as pools of light cascade from above: the cantor announces the opening psalm: his choir join him. As their phrase ends, they are answered promptly from the opposite side. And so the chanting is set up, an exchange of undulating Latin prayer which is passed backwards and forwards across the blank floor that divides the choirs.

At first, I was diffident to sing, anxious not to disrupt the chant or make a false note. I was an outsider among these practised professionals. Equally, it was hard at first to get my tongue around the Latin. But after a few days, I became confident as I was swept up into the boisterous noise. The experience is exhilarating, a group sharing its energy, men pooling their prayer force. For this was my initial surprise – how extremely prayerful yet physical chant is. The body language of bowing together, now sitting together, now rising, and all the while sustaining the chant backwards and forwards, knits the monks as one group. You are intensely aware of your neighbours on either side, especially the companion with whom you share the giant psalter; how they sit and how they sing; sometimes you clearly sense how they feel. You are more aware of the chant tone of your own team in contrast to the other side; yet there is a give and take all the while that sustains the rhythm of the whole body. Between the line breaks you wait for your echo to fall back down from the ceiling heights before completing with the second half of the verse. Once the chant is established, it has a living momentum of its own, ruled as much by the church acoustic as by the monks themselves. It is the swing and thrill of a rowing eight, the timeless rhythm of breakers on the shore.

31

Forbearance counts as much as stamina. A monk may stumble as he tries to fit the Latin words to the dipping line and from time to time a whole group fall off balance together. Still roped together, they grope their way to safety, finding the proper tone once more. When slips occur, a monk accepts his error publicly by kneeling down to kiss his psalter. This humble confession is offered by all ranks from novice monk to Prior. A further human failing proves inevitable. Ploughing to the end of lengthly psalms at dead of night, the tone must drop. Then, as the antiphon is repeated, signing off the psalm, all is revealed in a distinctly muddy swirl of sound. Then the knowing cantor cranks up a tone or two; and the new psalm breaks out afresh at proper pitch. It all makes for unremitting, steady work. Two hours of Matins with midnight passed.

The major portion of the Office is sung bottom-perched, comfortably enough, on the edge of the misericord, feet planted on the wood stringer that runs the length of the choir two feet out from the seats. No helping us. We all gaze down from time to time at this serried rank of feet thus planted and wonder at our being here. The choir seats are dropped, bums gracefully lowered when the singing ceases for a while and readers take their turn. Similar rest periods are claimed as both sides sit alternately as psalm sequences progress. (During Lent, however, such comforts are waived, and the entire Office is sung upright.) I could never work out their reckoning as these rests occurred, but was pleased to follow the general lead. Sat back now in your own stall, you are folded in an echo chamber so that you become aware of your individual voice as it is received into the choir.

Repeating the psalms year on year, the monk must become their familiar. He will find them one continuous, meaningful prayer. He does not so much attend to their words as to the overall message of the psalm, whether it is one of the great Messianic psalms which foreshadow Christ's sufferings and glory or one of the many appeals for God's help against the enemy, the psalms of entreaty, or one of the hymns praising God, often through the wonders of his creation. Sometimes a lapidary phrase sings out, such as the last words of Christ spoken on the cross; or something with another resonance completely, like the Magi coming from Sabah, their gifts in hand.

In my days on Fleet Street, there used to be a man who sat the long day through beside the news-tape. Known as the copy taster, his task was to spot important items as they broke and so alert the news desk right away. The same process takes place as we chant these psalms. It is never a question of making sense of each successive phrase as they are passed across from one choir to the other: rather, the threnody of prayer is sustained by red-hot embers of meaning which glow of their own accord upon the page and put warmth in each monk's heart. All the while, this re-enactment, our realization of an age-old prayer that goes back to David's day as once he sung God's praise in the Temple in thanksgiving for his Covenant with Israel. These are the very words which Christ himself prayed from his boyhood until the day he died. While overall hangs the lingering presence of the generations of monks who year upon year sat and prayed here on these same seats night after night, wielding these same great weighty books.

*

Some two thirds of the way through Matins comes a succession of readings, now from the Old Testament or perhaps from the Fathers. Chosen with great care, their effect can be electrifying. The one lengthly passage is broken into three to be shared by different readers. A chain of readings from Irenaeus were a revelation. His every word limpid, utterly fresh: in five hundred words he etches his point with cumulating clarity. He leads his audience with beguiling logic which he steadily unreels. He seems to possess some inner authority. Does it stem from his ancient Apostolic roots? Irenaeus, second-century Bishop of Lyons, scholar and martyr, was formed by Polycarp, who was himself bishop of Smyrna in Asia Minor. And Polycarp in his turn was a direct disciple of John the Apostle, living to a reverend age until the pagans burned him in their fires one day; it is from him that Irenaeus seems to draw that certainty in all he writes. His was our message night after night at two in the morning in the darkened church lit only by the lectern light and the steady red glow of sanctuary lights spluttering high against the roof.

By contrast, another night there came an extended reading from Ecclesiasticus that sent us into shivers. Culminating with 'Sin began with a woman, and thanks to her we all must die,' it is among the most misogynous passages in the entire Bible. It was a curious choice that I could only suppose was intended to sustain the monks in their chosen state of celibacy. Yet this was only a passing aberration.

Lauds follows on the heels of Matins, in lighter, more celebratory mood. With its great echoing canticle of praise, the Te Deum, it completes the night's business. Then the church is plunged once more in darkness, a Latin anthem to Our Lady is sung and the Angelus rings out in the church tower high above our weary heads.

I returned to my bed at 3.30 that morning, my whole senses full of the sounds and prayers sung, the liturgy of words read. The new experience still lay as physical memory somewhere across my chest. As I padded across the courtyard towards the guesthouse I remembered Eliot's words once more:

> You are not here to verify,
> Interest yourself, or inform curiosity
> Or carry report. You are here to kneel
> Where prayer has been valid.

III

SEEKING SOLITUDE

The highest and most sublime achievement in this life
is to remain still and let God act and speak in you.
Meister Eckhart

THE Carthusian seeks silence. He has entered the solitude of
his desert, that man-made seclusion that signals to himself
and to the outside world what he is about. He has gone there
to find God; or rather he comes to the desert of his innermost
self to permit God to find him. And his main path is the way of
silence.

It is important to understand true silence. Janus-faced, it
attracts and alarms us; and, at a deeper level, it has many
disguises.

There is the silence of deprivation that frightens us.
Teenagers seem to feel lost without their ghetto blaster, their
walkman, their insistent bonk-bonk music. Our discomfort
of being alone may last well into adult life, we still have not
learned how to become ourselves outside the warm womb.

There was a man shut in a lift between two floors (it was
reliably reported on Radio 3). His ordeal lasted over an hour.
At first he was relaxed; then he panicked, not knowing why. It
was only the next day that he was able to reflect upon his
experience with a friend: 'I know why I panicked: it was when
they switched off the muzak. Suddenly I knew I was alone.'
Alone with myself can be acutely painful.

There is another silence, the silence of absorption in
performing the task. Work may be said to become task in so
far as I succeed in making this activity my own. More readily,

we occupy our space in play and recreation, activities apart from work which we freely enjoy. The gardener absorbed in the season's job, the golfer making a good swing, the needle-worker finishing her design, a child lost in his play with building bricks. The accomplished sales person satisfying her customer's need, a deal well struck. When we are absorbed in the moment in this way, we speak of time well spent.

One Man and his Dog, a Welsh shepherd on TV: suddenly a jet roars overhead. Afterwards, the commentator asks how he succeeded in calming the sheep to carry them through the trial. 'I did not notice – plane, was it? I was too busy. But I saw the sheep looking!' We had seen the sheep lift their heads; they had been distracted: yet the shepherd had been bent to the silence of his task. It is the same silence that dissolves when suddenly we hear a clock's loud tick in a room that moments before we knew to be silent. But this stillness is not yet the silence of the desert.

I have been married for almost thirty years. My wife and I: husband and wife. We are also friends. It is a deep friendship that admits the wounds we each have scored upon the other. No perfection here. Our love has sustained this life together; the same love has also made us two different people since first we met. We have grown together: and that has enabled us to grow apart. One significant fruit of this living and growing together is our shared silence which sometimes breaks in. And frequently from that silence come shared thoughts. One of us will bridge the silence with words the other already knows. Call it thought reading, but there is a deeper reality: I am allowing the other into my being by my receptive silence of living love.

True silence is found in the heart, when one is present to oneself. No longer absence of sound, not simply a quenching of my thoughts and that great gamut of interior activity. True silence that can only come from within as I face myself.

I have a friend who once admitted that his chief distrac-tions in prayer were musical. I found myself impressed: musical distractions sounded of a higher order than my own tumble of mundane thoughts. I now know that my friend should have allowed his innermost silence to flood upwards and overwhelm his musical thoughts. Our life's task is to listen to this silence and allow it to rule our hearts. Here is true silence, the silence of the desert. It comes as a whisper from God and leads us on to him.

The Carthusian statutes invite 'quiet listening of the heart so that God may enter all its doors and passages'.

This silence permeates the charterhouse and gives us a first clue of its business. It takes all our ears to hear and hearts to understand its inner meaning.

*

Carthusians eat no breakfast. They break their fast each day with a main meal just before noon. But guests may cater for themselves in the guesthouse breakfast room, where there is an electric kettle, butter and fresh milk in the fridge, bread, cereals and biscuits. In the same narrow room with its dispro- portionately high ceiling and distracting echo lies a well- thumbed Visitors' Book dating back to September 1954. Unlike many another monastic community, Parkminster does not set out to be a retreat house. Visitors are discouraged, yet a steady trickle of visitors have passed through. During the forty years chronicled in the book, countless dozens of men have either visited for the afternoon or made a short stay with the Carthusians. Some few have wished to try their vocation, many others come in search of peace and prayer.

Leonard Cheshire was a regular visitor, staying almost every year since his first recorded visit in December 1954. He was a great admirer of the community and grew very close to them. Another regular name in the Visitors' Book is Thomas Merton's superior Dom James Fox, abbot of the Trappist monastery of Gethsemane in Vermont, celebrated in the fifties and sixties in Merton's many books. And the signatures of many other religious also pepper the Visitors' Book – Benedictines and Jesuits (mostly from Ireland), White Fathers, a Brother of St John of God as well as numerous Trappists and Carmelites. But the majority of visitors passing through are laymen of every kind. Two doctor brothers come together.

Groups of lads just out of school or still in the sixth form; almost certainly they come to work in the garden or bring in the cider apples from the cloister orchard. Two German brothers just out of school come from Dusseldorf; the younger brother Hans returns two years on and then is heard of no more. One lad signals his excitement at his experience of Parkminster: he records his name three times, entries made with mounting enthusiasm over a brief period of six weeks. At eighteen, he was too young to join the Order and is sent away for two years. His final message reads: 'Please God, in two years may I enter this house and never come out of it again.' He never returned: enthusiasm is the enemy of true self-knowledge. Visitors' nationalities are too numerous to detail: they range across every country in Europe and beyond: an Ibo from Nigeria is followed by a South African, men come from Burma and China, and yet more Benedictines from around the world – Mexico, Colombia and Ceylon.

The pilgrims could not be more diverse, yet their comments have a convergent ring, at once enthusiastic and naïvely touching. Every man that comes here has been profoundly moved. Comments such as 'wish I'd come years ago', 'a milestone in my life', 'unforgettable – how much is said in silence' reveal a message beyond human words that has passed time and again between these silent monks and their steady trickle of guests. Like moths, they have been drawn to this benign beacon of silence; far from being burned by some alien fire, they have returned home, fortified and refreshed.

A simple notebook purchased for ninepence from W. H. Smith fifty years ago is now well-thumbed, some pages loose, its binding in disarray. Yet it contains the eloquent testimony of decades of grateful visitors to Parkminster. Many return, regulars repeat their entries and witness the passing of the years. I find some names I remember at school, here again are boys I once taught. A sudden envy hits me: they have made their journey long ahead of me. 'Love bade me welcome, so I did sit and eat . . .' quotes one pilgrim. A Pole writes his thanks for the good advice he receives, others express astonishment at all that they have discovered. All speak of the hospitality of the monks, how they shared their home and above all their peace.

Men hear their silence and find it fills their hearts.

*

On my second evening, I was walking in the garden when I met Les, who had just arrived that afternoon for a two-night stay. He is not a Catholic, he told me, and only goes to church now and then: yet Les has been visiting Parkminster for over twenty years. He comes and gives his labour in return for the peace and silent companionship of the lay brothers. He is a paramedic and speaks enthusiastically about his profession. He knew that the evening ahead was going to be in silence and hard for him to endure. He confessed he was pleased to talk to me; yet all the while he knew Parkminster's very silence was why he came. He could not find the right words for his own experience; neither did he wonder what the monks were about in their daily routine. He had not come to pray with them; he was content simply to be briefly in their company. He was undemanding (indeed he had come to give), unquestioning yet implicitly grateful for all that he found rehabilitating in the unnameable experience of Parkminster.

The day I came away from the monastery I met the man who runs an art gallery some two or three miles distant. He took me down his garden to show me a nut walk. The prime purpose for its planting was to show off the nearby monastery. He was warmly enthusiastic about his neighbours; he had never visited but remained well content with their presence across the fields: 'I just like having them there,' was all he could say as he showed me the great rising spire surmounted by its cross.

Slowly I was building my perspective of the economy and sphere of influence of the Carthusian way of life. Yet I still had far to go to understand the meaning of their silent message. As prayer from their Office of Sext offers petitions:

O God, you know the secrets of hearts and never fail to hear our unspoken prayers. Help us to make our silence bear witness to your transcendent majesty. This we ask through Jesus Christ your Son, who with you and the Holy Spirit reigns One God for ever. Amen.

*

What brings a man to the Carthusian desert? What is he looking for? Once installed in his cell, how does he live? Is the day-to-day routine more or less identical? If so, how can he sustain such monotony, devoid of outside stimulus and with little or no recreation? I was full of such questions before I came to Parkminster; now that I was among them, I wanted some answers.

It will help to understand the Carthusian if we ignore his mediaeval trappings, since these are accidental to his purpose. Ignore for the moment the traditional white habit, the shaven heads, and the diet; these are certainly not peripheral to him, yet they present an immediate distraction to coming to know him. If the Japanese tourists only see the Trooping of the Colour, they may be excused for imagining that the Queen counts her guardsmen regularly as they march past her playing jolly tunes. We need to examine essentials.

Both before and after my visit to Parkminster, people would ask me: 'What are they doing?' To which I would reply lightly, almost to tease a reaction: 'They are praying for you and the world.' And then came the inevitable moment of confusion: 'But how much do they know of what is going on in the world?' Which is to mistake the nature of prayer. In fact, I found the community surprisingly well informed about world events, especially those areas bearing upon the life of the Church. There is no television or radio at Parkminster (yet they do have a fax!). There are two or three outside servants who work close to the community each day – Jonathan helps Benedict in the garden and Guy drives and works in the kitchen. They provide the source of major items of news. At the same time, the Prior gleans any major news items, both secular and religious, from a broadsheet newspaper and the Catholic weekly, *The Tablet*. And each week, Dom Bruno the Vicar (the Prior's deputy in his absence) pins up a sheet of suggested prayer intentions on the noticeboard outside church. They offer a kind of leper's squint to the outside world and are closely scrutinized by the community. They are wide-ranging and include world political events as well as personal intentions sent in by friends and relatives, a full spectrum of human concerns that preoccupy and affect the world at large.

Yet this is not why a monk exists. Prayer for the world is not their main concern: their first care is to confront God. Once in his presence, then prayer for and about the world flows as a matter of course.

From one perspective, a monk's true gift to the world could be seen as play. He seems an earnest enough fellow; yet consider his intentions. Like the lilies of the field, he neither reaps nor does he sow. He is a happy man, content to be where he is, living out his chosen life. Many of my readers would reply: I too would be happy if I knew that I had food and drink and a roof over my head for the remainder of my days. But it is not that simple. As the Belgian monk Ignace put it: 'Getting up at 12.00 for the Night Office, that's OK. The chastity, that's OK. The food and the hard bed, that's OK. But put them all together and that begins to get quite tough . . .'

The monk builds with simple bricks: his own daily failures, the infinite scale of his own aspirations, his faith that by God's given grace he may reconcile the two. He yearns for the God of Abraham and Isaac; he longs for Christ's promise, that he too may see the Father. He may have hungered in this way since youth, and the news of other men's encounters with God beckons him. Then comes the moment (and its experience is of many kinds) when he knows the imperative call to turn aside from the busy motorway of men. Leave the common wisdom of the world's ambitions, skills and achievements so that he may at last find what he has always hungered for.

To come to the nub of the Carthusian vocation: he is there in his cell not to pray for us but to forget himself in his search for God. This lifetime quest is never achieved until his brothers bear him to join the ninety who have already gone ahead to their Maker. He journeys without ambition. His new life is nothing less than an uncompromising love affair with the supremely loving and lovable God of the Trinity. In Cyril's words, the monk is God-struck and cannot help himself falling headlong into Christ's path. Time and again, I heard the sentiment announced by newcomers: I take it day by day, I only hope and pray that I can stay.

He joins this Carthusian way, in faith that others have gone before him and found successfully what he now seeks. He hopes he has been called by God to an intimacy that both acknowledges his Presence every minute of the day and invites him to a growing intimacy and loving service as the days become years.

This sense of discovery, the compelling excitement of finding Christ, not just as a notion but as a Person who transforms my life, is to be seen in the Gospel. John portrays it vividly. At the very start, the Evangelist creates three scenes as he describes how the first witnesses – himself among them – recognized Christ and were drawn at once into the mystery of his company. After the majestic simplicity of the prologue that spells out God's timeless commerce with man, John appears as witness to the imminent Christ. He baptizes the people with water, announcing his message of repentance in expectation of him who is to come. The next day, he sees Jesus walking directly towards him and says: 'Look, there is the Lamb of God that takes away the sin of the world.' He goes on to say that he himself did not recognize him until he saw 'the Spirit coming down on him from heaven like a dove'.

The third scene tells of the calling of the first disciples. The next day, John repeats his witness to his own disciples as Jesus again walks by. And now Andrew and a companion talk to Jesus, asking him where he lives. He replies with the simple invitation: 'Come and see.'

The story unfolds its own inner tension. Andrew tells his brother Peter: 'We have found the Messiah, the Christ.' And he takes Peter to Jesus, who says to him, 'You are Peter, son of John; you will be called Cephas, the Rock.' Then Christ calls Philip, who like Peter and Andrew is from the same town,

Bethsaida. Again the compelling imperative: 'Follow me.'

And now, like a stone skimming over the water, the good news passes rapidly from one friend to another. Philip seeks out Nathanael: 'We have found the one Moses wrote about in the Law, the one about whom the prophets spoke: he is Jesus, son of Joseph from Nazareth.'

'From Nazareth?' quips Nathanael. 'Can anything good come from that place?'

'Come and see,' echoes the reply. Now he too encounters Jesus, who at once recognizes that rare man of pure heart proclaimed in the psalms: 'This is an Israelite who deserves the name "incapable of deceit".' Nathanael asks Jesus how he knows him, and receives a reply that both astonishes and satisfies him by its intimate secrecy: 'Before Philip came to call you, I saw you under the fig tree.'

He in turn is compelled to express his open recognition of Jesus: 'Rabbi, you are the Son of God, you are King of Israel.'

Going back to this archetypal encounter between Christ and his first disciples, one sees the identical human response of today's contemplative. Like Philip, like Nathanael, there is the tension between being called and recognizing the compulsion of Christ's call. The 'Come and see', the 'Follow me' finds an echo of faith in the human heart and enables the disciple to sacrifice everything for the companionship of his Master.

It is the supreme yes: I know my Redeemer lives and I seize this chance, with both my hands. It becomes my own unique vision. Now I know how I want to commit my life.

*

The existential experience of joining any human group – be it the Brownies, the New Age Travellers, the public library, the tennis club – is that of identifying a path of new growth for myself within a group outside me. They have something I want. And by joining them, I hope to win these advantages. Some groups are more exclusive than others; they may seek to vet newcomers in order to limit the intake, so as to protect the overall well-being of the group and all that it stands for. The

Garrick Club has room for only one thousand members who, according to its rules, are men only and each approved as 'suitable' by the existing members. The Carthusian club is equally exclusive to a small core of men who share a special personal vision of Christ's work in the world.

The Carthusian vocation is both an affirmation of the reality of God's redeeming work in Christ and a rare statement of man's possible response. The silent witness speaks to the world outside of the whole economy of salvation. Their motto *'In Cruce mundo'* is expressed by the icon of the Carthusian cross: a circle, the world, supports the cross. Or is it otherwise: the interstices break through the circle of the world to overcome its embrace? Yet at the same time, the circle locks the cruciform, making it stronger than ever. There is no life without the cross: Christ by his cross gives new life to the world.

*

It is hard not to admire the initial beauty of Bruno's ideal: more remarkably, his fragile dream of creating an island Utopia in pursuit of God has lasted through nine centuries of human existence. His own account is persuasive. Supremely gifted, the most accomplished scholar in the Christian world of his day, a balanced and integrated man who attracted everyone who met him, Bruno was at the same time a brilliant administrator, ambassador and statesman. For over twenty years, he was chancellor of one of the major seats of learning of the time, the cathedral school of Rheims; he had taught two generations of some of Europe's finest scholars, including princes, bishops and the future Pope Urban II. Suddenly he falls out of favour with the new bishop and, losing everything – position, power and money – he goes into exile with a small group of friends.

We have his own account of his conversion to the solitary life in one of only two extant letters in his hand. He had come together with two close friends in the 'little garden beside Adam's house', he writes – that is, with Raoul (later Dean of Rheims and the recipient of this same letter) and the surreally named Fulk the one-eyed. And their talk was all about their present predicament. Three men committed to the truth and wishing to serve Christ and his Church find their way barred by men of the world. Their solution was but one short step away: to leave the world and create a hidden haven of their own. In Bruno's words:

> I remember only too well. We had been discussing at great length the empty attractions, the passing riches of this present life as compared to the joy of eternal glory. As it turned out, we became more and more enthusiastic and our hearts began to race with God's love: at length we three promised, resolved – vowed even – to turn our backs on this world of passing shadows as soon as we may and grasp hold of the eternal by taking the monastic habit.

In other words, these three good men had had enough of pitting themselves against the visible world they had long known. The time had come, they saw clearly, to retreat into a world that recognized only God's timeless plan. They would become monks.

Only Bruno followed through; he failed to carry his two friends with him on his journey to the desert. Perhaps they felt daunted by the heroic simplicity of Bruno's vision. Yet viewed across the centuries, one has to admire its clear simplicity. He devised – and his followers subsequently refined – a unique response to God's eternal invitation to man. It was to be a secret way, completely hidden from the world in mute defiance of the worst it had to hurl at them. His way was to seek God as a solitary within the loving security of community: so rarified a call that it would elude all but a handful over the centuries.

Bruno avoided creating a selfish Utopia by settling his first companions in log huts on a remote and inhospitable mountainside in Gaul. The site was so harsh and extreme that an early avalanche swept the first settlement away with loss of life. And a new monastery had to be re-sited lower down.

Surely any man alive would step onto a hillside to find his

God. That was certainly the way he saw it. The purpose of his letter to Raoul (written years later) was to remind him of his promise in Adam's garden and persuade him to fulfil it by at last joining him in distant Calabria, the site of his second monastery:

> I am living in the wilderness of Calabria, far removed from habitation. There are some brethren with me, some of whom are very well educated, and they keep constant watch for their Lord, so as to open to him at once when he knocks. I could never even begin to tell you how charming and pleasant it is. The temperatures are mild, the air healthy; a broad valley, a delight to the eye, reaches from one mountain peak to the other along their whole length. It is quite filled with fields and meadows that boast all manner of sweet-smelling herbs and flowers. The impact of these gently undulating hills all around with their folded valleys in between through which flow a variety of brooks and streams is quite indescribable. And for good measure, we ourselves have an abundance of lush gardens that boast every kind of fruit tree.

In Adam's garden, he had taken critical issue with his known world; in the eyes of the majority of his contemporaries he had taken a terrible fall. As events unfolded, Bruno was soon back in Rheims, rehabilitated, even promoted to replace his former foe as bishop elect. But he would have none of it. His mind was set.

He wanted to travel a new road. His loadstone was poverty and complete forgetfulness of self. He had turned away from all he had known and begun a new journey. Yet it was a journey not entirely of his own planning. Like Christ's warning to Peter, he was to be diverted from his purpose against his own will.

> As a young man, you went where you pleased.
> As an old man, another will lead you where you would rather not go.

46

Bruno and his first companions had no sooner established themselves in rough log cabins perched in the winter snows high above Grenoble, than their founder was summoned away on the Pope's business. His former pupil at Rheims, now Pope Urban II, was beset with the complex business of running the Church; he turned to his mentor for help. Bruno never saw his first retreat at La Grande Chartreuse again, but died in a second foundation in distant Calabria, the despised heel of Italy. His first urge to create a solitude in order to find God had been turned upon its head: God had led him along a strange and unmapped route. But it had led home all the same.

The news that a score of white-robed, neighbouring monks perform the same daily tasks and spiritual duties that Bruno and his companions enacted all those years ago on a mountainside in Calabria would astonish the citizens of Brighton, should they ever happen upon such information. The Carthusians have survived because their principal task is as valid today as when Bruno enunciated it long ago in Adam's small garden. Man hungers for God, whom he must find. The search will always continue in a special solitude apart from other men's eyes.

IV

THE MYSTIC CHRIST

I have been crucified with Christ, and I live now
not with my own life but with the life of Christ
who lives in me.
  Galatians 2:19–20

THERE is a strangely haunting passage in St Exupery's allegory, *Le Petit Prince*, when the fox suggests that the Little Prince should tame him. The fox is wild; he runs from men, since most are interested in shooting him. Taming, he explains, is a delicate business, but the rules are straightforward. At the same time each day, the Little Prince must come to the same place each day and sit watching the fox. And each day the fox watches the Little Prince – out of the corner of his eye. Until one day the Little Prince knows that he has tamed his Fox: now at last they can be friends. 'You can only know someone when you have tamed them,' explains the fox.

So it was over a period of weeks that I first observed the community, as no doubt they observed me. I saw them come to church on time and smile as they passed the bell rope one to the other. I watched their patient observance, their reverent performance of the Office in their vigil night after night and again in the late afternoon. I attended their Eucharist, the silent powerhouse of their day. I saw men pray who were journeying to God. I saw men attending to their self-imposed sacred duties with all the pure, earnest attention of children at play. I worked with the brothers as they performed all manner of tasks: cultivate the garden and prepare their meals, tend their sick and offer loving care to the old men.

As I shared their daily routine, trying to join in with like

48

spirit, I recognized men of great patience and considerable love. Parkminster was not the first religious house I had lived in; I was able to measure it against many others I had known. Here I found something rare and special, a core desire to perform each day's tasks, both work and prayer, as simply and as perfectly as possible. I am not describing piety or pompous show – or even a recessive meekness. I tell of all manner of mature men taking their day seriously and steadily in order to carry out its demands with an impressive mix of joy and perseverance.

*

The first surprise about the men of Parkminster is their international identity. Known as the English-speaking community, it seems that almost no Englishman is there to be found and counted. Instead, they come from Poland and Slovakia; from Switzerland and Belgium; from Australia and the Philippines; from Nigeria and from Holland by way of South Africa . . . And finally you do at last spy an Englishman, a Scotsman – and now an Irishman or two.

Looking back on the history of Parkminster, it was always so. The original monks were in the main French but were later joined by a second influx of exiled Germans. There was a steady trickle of Irish, but always fewer Englishmen came to try the life. In France, after an exile of almost half a century, monks returned to La Grande Chartreuse in the dark, uncertain days of Vichy France. And here, after the vicissitudes of war, the community has flourished with a steady flow of native French vocations. The pattern of recruitment in England has been far less vigorous. Predictably, there was a bulge just after the war; but since then few have persevered. Today there is a yawning gap between the older members of the community, now in their seventies, and the new arrivals, young men of twenty to thirty. Recently, in an attempt to revive this ageing community which at times must have seemed doomed to terminal decline, European and English-speaking postulants worldwide have been diverted to the Engilsh charterhouse. The international mix gives the community a certain modern zing, putting one in mind of a modern university or the Sussex bureau of a large multi-national company. Still small in number – hovering around the twenty-five mark – the Parkminster community represents a wide geographic range of culture as well as professional backgrounds. There are soldiers and sailors, a doctor, a prison governor, a professional musician and more than one computer programmer: between them they possess a broad bank of experience of the world that as individuals they have chosen to leave behind.

*

It is always glibly tempting to judge a contemplative as a fugitive from reality: the nun has neatly solved her problems about sexuality; the monk has abandoned all serious commitment to the rich feast of life.

To possess an outstanding musical gift only to turn one's back on your international audience, to leave a busy parish in Warsaw precisely at its time of crisis: such decisions seem wholly negative. Why didn't Brother Augustine continue to teach in his South African township school? Should not Dom Bernard have stayed on after he was serving the community as their family doctor? The crossroad for the contemplative comes when, in reaching out unequivocally towards his God, he seems to turn his back on mankind.

Yet nothing is further from the truth. If his journey is successful, he will have laid foot on another area of human experience. Holiness, or rather the human journey towards God, must count as important to every man. And all are benefited by the undertaking, whatever the measure of success of each individual's journey.

The contemplative takes Christ for his model, whose mission in life he seeks to follow: son of a carpenter who spent his entire life as an obscure and unknown country bumpkin. At length, when he did emerge people were heard to whisper – 'From Nazareth, is he, of all places?' And this public moment, when at last it came, was completely eclipsed by the marvels being performed by John the Baptist. When John was dead, and fresh wonder-stories continued circulating in Galilee,

Herod's reaction was to suppose that the Baptist had come back to life.

It is from St John's Gospel that we receive the fullest statement of the nature of the Son's mysterious business from the Father which tracked Christ all his life:

No one can come to the Father except through me.
If you know me, you know my Father too.
From this moment you know him and have seen him . . .
To have seen me is to have seen the Father.
John 14:6–7, 9

When you have lifted up the Son of Man,
then you will know that I am He
and that I do nothing of myself:
what the Father has taught me
is what I preach;
he who sent me is with me,
and has not left me to myself,
for I always do what pleases him.
John 8:28–29

This is Christ's purpose: to bring man into the previously unknown obscurity of the Father. His message is never his own; it is as if he is always looking over his shoulder towards his Father, whom he must communicate and give full account of to men before returning to him. In this sense, Christ is the Mystic *par excellence* who comes to man in order to speak of the Father and set his redemptive plan in motion. He did this by his death and resurrection, acts by which he mothered the Church, drawing all men into the love life of the Trinity through the enabling gift of his grace.

Now the contemplative is drawn into this same task by Christ's call. Like Christ, he too must first die. This is the inner meaning of his abnegating vows. Those three pledges could not be more calculated to seal a man's fate in the world's eyes. Yet they are the instruments, the three nails by which he gives over his life's most treasured ambitions. A

51

chaste man, he surrenders what is most dear to men: a wife and above all children. A poor man, he hands over all his present goods and abdicates all future right to all possessions and riches. Obediently he seeks to imitate Christ, who was 'always doing what most pleases the Father'.

The death that follows is but the cipher of resurrection that opens our eyes to Christ's majestic gift to man: his own new life – a unique invitation – to be achieved within each individual.

We can recognize the contemplative as a man in Christ's image called to die to himself in order to live more fully in the knowledge of the Father. Rather than dying in life, he now lives out his death, day by day. Life is brought to the boil by seizing death's initiative. As St Paul sings: 'I am dead to the Law, so that now I can live for God. I have been crucified with Christ, and I live now not with my own life but with the life of Christ who lives in me.' Galatians 2:19–20

The contemplative enters this contract with God as Christ did – for and on behalf of all men. It is not a selfish act, but an act of love that flows outwards, part of Christ's love to us all.

V

THE MEN BENEATH THE COWL

Yet God ...
Could crowd career with conquest while there went
Those years and years by of world without event
That in Majorca Alfonso watched the door.
Gerard Manley Hopkins

BROTHER Richard is porter. Like Alphonsus Rodriguez, the Jesuit lay brother whom Hopkins praises for his fifty years of duty in Majorca, he too keeps the door. And that unchanging routine affords God power to change him. It was Richard who opened the door to me on my first visit to Parkminster, taking me by surprise when he passed the time of day as we marched off together to find the Prior. Now after my first Vespers, he smiled at me as we negotiated the large wood-partition door that divides the cloister from the brothers' quarters and the guesthouse.

'Where are you from?' he asked. I told him Taunton. Whereupon he was back fifty years just after the war, doing his Military Service in the town's Jellalabad Barracks.

'I don't suppose they still have the Somerset Light Infantry any more?' he asked. I replied that I wouldn't be surprised to learn that they had been disbanded. From now on I was simply known as 'Taunton' to Brother Richard.

In many ways my first Carthusian encounter with Richard stands for all the rest. Here is a totally unremarkable man. A Lancastrian ex-soldier who somehow found his way to Parkminster. Years on, he is still there, but how much has changed: the community cite him as an example of how the rhythm of the life can make a man.

Minding the gate of a charterhouse, like counting swallows

on Boxing Day, can hardly be the most exacting of tasks. Few come and fewer go. But these duties are rotated and three months on, Richard is helping to nurse the two invalids, Dom Moraes and Brother Gabriel, now confined to their cells by terminal sickness.

Like many religious establishments, the charterhouse is at first sight two communities, the choir monks and the brothers (or *conversi*). It is an ancient arrangement that goes back to days when gentlemen needed servants to cook and care for them. All that seemed a good idea at the time and perdured over the centuries. Only recently has it been critically examined and found wanting. Not surprisingly, it has taken a deal of unscrambling after standing in place all that while. My experience of the Jesuits was that in modern times there has been only a very small intake of brothers. With their defined role as servant and little attempt to afford modern professional training, few recruits were attracted and those who came were all too easily treated as second-class citizens. But reforms triggered by the Second Vatican Council are changing such attitudes.

Nowadays, brothers are fully integrated members of the community. They sit alongside the choir monks and join in singing the Office (although some still prefer to remain passive participants); they also take their turn to read the lessons. Several now live in the cloister hermitages, previously the exclusive preserve of choir monks, an innovation that represents a remarkable departure from past norms, when brothers were either billeted in rooms along the corridor above the kitchen (where there is little privacy or silence) or, the better option, in cells in the obedience yard.

Saint Bruno was an imaginative pioneer, who was to establish a revolutionary new model of strict monastic life – that of hermits living in community. Moreover, it was all to happen in the 'desert' of a remote French mountainside. Choosing men well endowed with the practical skills essential to this task must have seemed a necessity. Bruno's boldness in siting La Grande Chartreuse halfway upon a mountain, as we have already seen, was put in doubt when an avalanche later swept through the log cabins and several lives were lost. One did not venture into this kind of wilderness without good engineers.

Pioneers are one thing, hewers of wood and drawers of water another. But this latter role has been long overplayed. Somewhere along the line one would have expected that the appearance of Caxton and the subsequent revolution in education might have impinged. For centuries now *conversi* have all to a man been able to read and write in addition to their skills as cooks, tailors and menders of tractors. Yet somehow no one noticed.

When the plans for Parkminster were drawn up in the middle of the last century, the architect's brief was to house two distinct communities, the one supporting the other. As a result, the brothers had their own chapel, their own refectory – even a separate chapter house. And when they came to church, it was to kneel apart in the lower half of the church telling their rosary beads, while the choir monks – rendered invisible behind a barrier more solid than any cathedral rood screen – performed the Latin Office in the main body of the church.

There is nothing too sinister about this original dispensation. Indeed, it is clear from one of only two extant letters written by Bruno how much he admired and valued the brothers of La Grande Chartreuse as he received word of them in distant Calabria at the second charterhouse he had established. It was simply a question of those monks who could neither read nor write being offered useful tasks within the charterhouse. It was only sad that it had to last so long, due chiefly to the divisiveness of Latin being used exclusively in singing the Office.

One sad episode in the Annals of Parkminster illustrates how one brother grew to resent his treatment by the system, until he finally became alienated. As the century turns, Brother X has been a member of the community for over twenty years. He has held all key offices in succession – tailor, cook, gardener. Yet he steadily grows dissatisfied. He begins to feel the community, even his superior, does not offer him esteem. The official records give no clue as to the detailed negotiations that must have passed between brother and Prior. Awareness must have matched alarm on both sides. Now of a sudden, he appeals directly to the Pope for dispensation from his vows, this at the time of the Modernist crisis when there can have been little truck or sympathy for his cause in Rome. Eventually, he is allowed to leave the Order but only on condition that he continues to observe his vows and agrees to wear distinguishing clerical dress. The poor, angry man ends up in a nearby workhouse, a sad victim of the system breaking down upon the head of the individual.

*

At Parkminster they say: 'The choir monks don't do very much and the brothers help them do it.' Behind the jest may hide a morsel of truth. The brothers maintain the working wheels of the monastery in its daily routine to afford the choir monks their solitude and to enable them to have freedom to follow their spiritual rota.

The two exceptions are Prior and Procurator, whose invidious task it is to maintain a hermit's life while seeing to the strategic and everyday running of the monastery. The Procurator links the monastery with the outside world, buying in food and every material necessity. His task, akin to that of the bursar of an Oxford college, becomes onerous when the man in question had come to the monastery to pray. Definitely the nightmare short straw for any Carthusian.

Ten times more hard to bear is the lot of the Prior, who is charged with the well-being of the entire community. Not only, as soul doctor, does he take intimate cure of each member of the community, but in his hands alone is the forward planning of the physical survival of the group. What he decides goes. We are dealing here with a neo-monarchy, if it were not for the regular intervention of the visitation. Every other year two outside visitors arrive from separate charter-houses and perform a thorough spiritual and temporal audit. Such routine practice may have led to the quiet boast of the Order, 'never deformed, never reformed'. But the reality behind never becoming deformed is nine hundred years of continuous fidelity to the on-going spirit of Bruno; to be exact, it is the sum of the regimental loyalty of each individual, whose day to day fidelity to the duty of their calling has built a living, interlocking wall stretching back and forward all those centuries.

The earliest Carthusian vow format prayed for the new monk as he joined the body of the community: 'that he may recognize Christ in order not to run behind the others, nor to listen to their voice, but rather to Yours saying "Who wishes to serve me, let him follow me."'

*

Today it still remains for the brothers to cook, clean, garden and take charge of every general task. Their skills span the repair of machinery to horticulture. Bee-keeping and cider-making still flourish, skills passed down the generations within the community. Tailoring and printing have been lost, their passing witnessed by great empty tombs: the print shop with its multiplicity of types still neatly kept aslant, as if inviting the setter still to do one last bite of type before night falls. The tailor shop, too, is faded, dusty now, its stained lights above the gatehouse lacklustre, as if they have lost all hope of seeing it in use once more.

Manpower is in short supply. The tasks are endless. And prayer cuts across each day. Thus the weeds grow between the flags, grass musters, box hedge stands ten foot high.

Only essential jobs get done. There are the sick to nurse, confined to their cells. A watchful eye must be kept on those, ancient of days, who still roam the cloister: *item*, Brother Christopher, whom we will shortly encounter. It was exclusively brothers I first met when I joined them each afternoon in the kitchen or at work in the garden; only later would I get to know the choir monks, one or two by chance encounter and then all at once on my final day when I was permitted to join the community walk on their Monday outing.

Silence dominates Parkminster. It is each monk's *leitmotif*, the cipher of his inner solitude, a second silence beyond the physical barrier propounded by external rule. The brother's

silence needs to be even more robustly observed than that of
the choir monk in his hermitage; his ideal will be that his day's
work becomes his means of constant prayer. In spite of this,
silence is by no means absolute; its observance is subtle. If a
task has to be done, there is no recourse to intermediary sign
language such as that used until recently by Trappists.
Necessary talk is conducted in a normal, surprisingly relaxed
manner, but is kept to an economic minimum. One soon
becomes aware, however, of the delicate tension between the
solitary, eremetic life and its context within a supportive
community. Such conversations are never garrulous, yet
neither are they cut short by some pious guillotine. (I was
impressed on first meeting the Prior at how timeless our
conversation seemed. I was presenting him with a decision to
be made: the premise was, let us both take the time needed to
reach a good conclusion.) Throughout my stay, I found
immense courtesy and kind consideration at every turn. More
than mere human courtesy; I felt genuinely received and
welcomed as an honorary member of the group. These men
know how to love: and they express it in their use of time.

Ignatius ran the kitchen; and I reported to him for my work
period at one o'clock each afternoon. He is Spanish and was
prior in one of the five charterhouses in his country when his
health gave way. After a period of uncertainty and painful
recovery, he obtained leave to come to England as a brother,
although he still says Mass privately. He is a tall man, big-
boned with an interior smile. You feel that he deliberates well
on all he does. He took me aside at once and asked me if I
understood about silence. In spite of my ready affirmative, he
went ahead with his own definition as if to lay his firm
ground-rules. He summed them up as follows: 'We can talk
because of the job but nothing else; then we are silent.' His
English is more than adequate, but he remains diffident about
his skills. He has all those lovely shuffled consonants so
peculiar to the Spanish tongue as it bravely tries to wrap itself
around an endless succession of English words. When he
gives you a job in his kitchen, he finds it simpler to mime the
first few stages until he is confident that you understand

exactly what he needs. His stout defence of silence in his domain is underlined by a large notice – evilly printed upon a yellow background – that announces a complete set of rules, as if for some ancient courtly game such as croquet or real tennis: 'Silence is to be observed at all times in the kitchen except when a new task is being detailed . . . Conversations should be kept to a minimum and should only pertain to work in hand . . . No whistling. No singing . . .' His strict ideals were no surprise, and from the start, I enjoyed working with him.

My first task was to attack the pots in a back-breaking *plongeur's* sink which enabled me to feel heroically penitent. (Yet I could not refrain from cursing its designer, wondering whether he had ever worked his diabolical device.) Beside me worked a postulant brother, a Filipino, who with a warm smile introduced himself as Neil; only later did I know him properly as Joseph, his chosen name in religion. Another companion in the kitchen was a layman I had seen opposite me in choir. Working the dish-washer – a sturdy, noisome machine – he introduced himself as John and explained that, now he was retired, he spent the inside of his week, Monday to Friday, at Parkminster. His proudest duty was to polish and dust the church every Monday; the rest of the week, he spent in the kitchen. He has a deep affection for the community as well as for the buildings of Parkminster and was a valuable source of detailed information. His status as lay-helper is not unusual. The library is cared for by Gordon, a retired businessman and Carthusian buff, who spends the majority of his time at Parkminster but is free to come and go. A step further than this lay-helper status (known as a 'familiar') is that of donate. He is a dedicated man who has joined the Order and keeps the rule in every detail, but who for a variety of reasons (most frequently 'health' – perhaps he cannot sustain the rigours of the Night Office) has not been allowed to take the habit. Only in exceptional circumstances are men over forty admitted to full profession; it is felt that by that age, they may not be capable of the full inner change that is to be expected in a younger man.

After cleaning the pots, I was asked to mince about two pounds of Dutch cheese to go into mashed potatoes, to augment their nutritional punch. I marvelled at the vintage machine that was asked to perform this job; it required considerable persuasion after what had clearly been long years of public service. I wondered whether the older monks, now decades on at Parkminster, felt a similar difficulty, perhaps a spiritual stiffening in their joints, or was their life made easier by continuous daily practice?

Next, the preparation of twenty-three salads for supper in small brown earthenware dishes. The afternoon's work was nearly done. It was time for Joseph to wash the floor. First he sprayed and wiped all the working surfaces with the thoroughness of a surgeon about to cut into his patient's abdomen. Then he started on the floor. This activity soon held me mesmerized. He was only washing a kitchen floor; what could possibly be remarkable in that? Every inch was patiently and scrupulously covered. He worked an elaborate galvanized bucket set upon wheels, with a special lever mechanism to press out the dirty water. His meticulous care, the kind purpose in his whole body as he leaned upon the mop or rinsed it time and again, transformed his mundane work into a unique act of prayer.

I was not in the least surprised to find Joseph's head cropped and himself fully clothed in the black and white novice's habit when three month's later I rejoined the community for a second spell. I was to learn the story of how Joseph came to Parkminster on the weekly walk. But I already admired his style.

We had nearly finished when another monk came into the kitchen from working in the garden. (No wonder Ignatius had hung his Silence notice: the kitchen can so easily become a meeting point.)

'How do you do. I am Benedict.' This was delivered in a direct and simple manner. We shook hands. Benedict is head gardener. His endearing ways are thoroughly recognizable as from the English counties, in both accent and mien. He has abundant humour that illumines his approach to religious life. He stands five foot seven, has a tumbled white beard, glasses and prominent hearing aids. The twinkle never leaves his eyes. I took out instant membership in Benedict's fan club.

As I came to the end of my kitchen duties, Brother Ignatius showed me the shower room just inside the back door. This was indeed great news. I had sploshed cold water over myself from a hand basin in a drafty guesthouse loo that morning, followed by a shave in cold water using the ewer and basin in my room – an arrangement that took me back to the primitive days of my Jesuit noviceship. Now this was some surprise: real Carthusian luxury, a hot shower on the ground floor of a large house: from now on, I could be confident of a good delivery of hot water each morning. Gradually all life's mysteries were beginning to be solved.

The next morning at 10.30 with 'Manual Work' listed on my timetable, I thought I might redeem the kitchen herb garden that runs along outside the scullery window. I had seen it choked with a season's weeds the day before: some sort of service to Ignatius for his gentleness was suggested. I sought out Benedict in the kitchen garden, through the wall on the far side of the yard. I found him bent over an ancient hand plough which he was propelling slowly along the length of a carrot drill. His purpose seemed to be to remove weeds, but I did not see fit to question him. He greeted my suggestion of the herb garden with enthusiasm and came to give me a tour of the herbs (courteously identifying weeds from herbs and adding rocket to my vocabulary of recognition). He told me which to cut back and which to favour.

It was an extensive herb garden and it took me three work sessions each morning to make my mark. The Carthusian day – just like school – is a succession of short measured periods joined end to end spanning the day. To achieve anything you must learn how to put the same task together at the same time day after day. Thus the simple task of weeding my herb patch from 10.30 until 11.15 (when the bell sounds for Sexts) becomes a calculated operation. You must first get down to the tool cellar to select wheelbarrow, fork, secateurs, hoe, yard broom. Next proceed to site. Five minutes before the end of the allotted period, allow time to sweep up, empty barrow and return all tools to their place in the cellar. Job productivity is necessarily curtailed. Possibly if I had been a choir monk, everything would have been to hand. I could have tilled my lettuce, turned a chair leg or continued carving my Madonna using the time allotted to the full.

The day is broken so as to enable the monk to move through it in the Presence of God: now he prays the Office, now he reads; he works to relieve the mind and uses his body while his heart stays with the Spirit. He eats his meal alone and without rush, digesting the day so far and mulling over his thoughts and aspirations. Afterwards he may pick up his Bible and read a passage slowly in the manner known as *lectio Divina* – a contemplative way of sucking the meaning by association, almost welcoming discursive thoughts that carry one's mind to a deeper level of understanding and enrichment.

The brother too is a praying man all his livelong day. He peels his potatoes, hoes his line of carrots, washes and dresses the bedridden Dom Moraes: but as he does so, he too is with God, deepening his experience of encounter day by day.

The questing journey continues.

*

On my second day, I was surprised when Ignatius apologized for his mashed potatoes that had been served that day. I replied that I thought they had been quite acceptable, but he insisted that they had gone bad and that some monks had returned them uneaten. The next day, Ignatius was not in the kitchen. I was told he had a guest and was therefore off duty. (Summer is the time for family visits and there were several during my stay.) But by the third day, as Benedict took over cook's duties as well as continuing to run the garden, it became clear that Ignatius had succumbed to another of his periodic bouts of nervous tension. When I returned to Parkminster for my second visit, I learned that Ignatius had returned home to Spain for good.

The stress on the contemplative is ever present. One might imagine that the question, 'Is this the life for me?' would be resolved within the first six months in the monastery. But it is a question that can pose itself of a sudden after years of apparent stability and progress as a monk. When it bubbles up to the surface, the community lends support as best it can. But it can easily erupt without warning. Several years back, one of the lay brothers had been working on a building project. He was driving tractor and trailor with a load of bricks when something suddenly snapped. Hours later, the police telephoned.

'Is that Parkminster? We have one of your monks in custody. He was driving a tractor through Guildford with a load of bricks. He is not insured and neither he nor his vehicle has a licence.'

The runaway monk trailing his load of bricks was widely reported – even as far away as New Zealand. The prior wrote an apologetic account of the stress and strains of Carthusian life in the Catholic press. The culprit pleaded as much before the magistrate and was treated lightly. He had made his point: he is now married with two children and drives a bus in Glasgow.

I asked the Prior if professional help was ever sought in such cases. He replied with an emphatic yes, adding that one did not play with fire.

*

The benign regime of Benedict running the kitchen contrasted with that of Ignatius. I was promoted in the creative hierarchy (which left Benedict back in the sink). An eighteen-egg omelette was the order of the day. When I protested 'not all at once', I was overruled by Holy Obedience. I was musing on this gigantic novelty, all of a sizzle in the great frying pan, when Benedict returned. My face must have been solemn, because he insisted that I cheer up. And from then on, he set out to keep my spirits on the up with a regular sally of monkish jokes.

'Did you hear about the Benedictine novice at Douai? "Now I'm very glad you asked me about the Trinity: I seem to be the only one around here who understands how it works."'

Then there was the tale about when Brother Andrew died.

'We daren't tell him that one,' glances exchanged. By way of encouragement I offered my story of the six-foot-four Jesuit who, when it came to plant him, was too long for his grave: nothing could persuade him to fit. Our burial party had to leave him wedged, half in, half out, until the grave-diggers returned to accommodate him.

The problem was the contrary with Brother Andrew, but again a solution was to hand. The Carthusian is afforded no coffin but is quite simply laid out in his best habit upon a plank. After the Requiem Mass, he is taken from the church to be buried in the bare earth just as he is.

The carpenter at the time would only provide planks six foot six long; whereas Brother Andrew was a mere five foot six. The ground was hard at the time and, since the statutory grave depth was a generous six foot under, something had to be done. The answer was simple. Taking a saw into the church, the offending plank was reduced to a sensible and fitting size. Brother Andrew was not heard to complain.

More funeral stories followed. A monk from Sussex died and numerous local relatives attended his send-off in the Priory church. There was some concern to count heads accurately so that all the guests would be adequately catered for after the Mass and burial. One brother was convinced that Benedict, who as acolyte was wielding a thurible to generate incense, had not been alerted to two late arrivals. So each time he passed, he hissed and raised two discreet fingers. Benedict ignored him, since he knew the correct tally full well; which only led to more urgent two finger signalling from the anxious monk.

Afterwards there was a discussion about this unseemly scene. The question was how would the visitors – many of them not Catholics – have interpreted such signals. Benedict was told, 'I expect, Brother, they just thought he didn't like you very much.'

*

The history of each monk is as distinct as it is fascinating. My own theory on the psychological background of a person called to religion is that there is not infrequently an absent father for the man and a very present father for the woman. (St Thérèse of Liseux adored her father, yet leaving him for the convent, was able to use his image to further her journey to Christ.) The majority of men known to me who have become priests have either had no father, or an absent or recessive father. It is as if the journey into religious life takes over the quest for the father. I have no difficulty with this model: from the soil of human experience comes new growth. Death brings resurrection; God works this way.

Benedict joined the merchant navy during the last war at the age of seventeen. He served as a wireless operator on the Atlantic convoys. In one sally, I had said, 'If they ever let you guys out, you will have to be completely re-educated – learn the meanings of words like nylons . . .' I was interrupted to be told that when I was still in short trousers, he had been a sailor.

'We brought nylons home from America wound around our bodies – quite against the rules – and they weren't all for Mum!'

After the war, he studied electrical engineering and joined a successful company. But then he made a retreat with the Benedictines at Prinknash and became fascinated. His former fast ways seemed empty. He joined as a lay brother, not wishing to become a priest. He stayed three years and then turned to the Carthusians to fulfil his desire for a stricter way of life. Benedict has been a religious for forty-four years. He oversees the garden, and now currently the kitchen; he also finds time to tend the hives, which house a particularly vicious breed of German bee. And for good measure, he is also the house electrician.

*

When the Prior had first briefed me on my arrival at Parkminster, he had given me a key which he referred to as a *passepartout*. I would need it to get through into the church cloisters from the guesthouse. The significance of this only became apparent when I first bumped into Brother Christopher outside the kitchen door.

To enter the kitchen, you use a cylinder key that hangs on a chain from the door jamb outside. I was collecting my lunch on my second day when I found the old lay brother standing on the threshhold looking somewhat lost. I side-stepped and opened the door, wondering if it was beyond his capabilities. I held it open for him to come through; but instead Ignatius shooed him away and closed the door firmly. I took my lunch box and left by the back door, still wondering what was going on.

Christopher's life story is the most dramatic of any monk at Parkminster. The son of a Polish railway worker, he was born just after the turn of the century. During the First World War, his town was overrun by the Russian army, who ruthlessly pressed every fit man into forced labour. While he was still a lad, his family was split up and taken off to Siberia. But in the disorder created by the Bolshevik Revolution of 1917, Christopher, still only fifteen, managed to escape back to Poland. When he was of age, he joined the Polish army and later married. During the Second World War, his wife, who was involved in the Resistance, was arrested and killed by the Gestapo. Christopher himself served as a tank driver with the Polish Armoured Division that landed in Europe shortly after D-Day to play a critical part in the advance into Germany. In the thick of the Normandy battles, he contrived to visit the basilica of St Thérèse at Lisieux, and here, to his confusion and surprise, he felt a strong desire to become a monk.

At the end of the war, his first thoughts were to find his wife and bring her out of Poland, now once again overrun by the Russian 'liberating' army. Taking an army truck and a case of whisky, Christopher trekked across the length of post-war Europe and into Poland. Here he learned of his wife's fate; there was little he could do, and he had already resolved to quit his native land. But he was anxious about the fate of a family of close friends, so he set off to their rescue. Having successfully located them, he persuaded them of his plan to flee the country. The whisky worked wonders to bribe the Russian soldiers manning the frontiers, and the entire party succeeded in reaching England safely. Christopher now attended to his own unfinished business. Under the guidance of a Polish priest, he made two retreats to find out more about the religious life, one with the Benedictines, the other with the Carthusians. The Carthusians drew him in.

For many years, Christopher was cook at Parkminster. I had already heard tales of his culinary skills from Les, who was the first to tell me his wartime saga. Whenever Les came in from the garden, Christopher would ask what he wanted to eat and then provide a meal of generous proportions. His regular refrain was: 'I've been cooking here for a hundred years.'

The Christopher of today is completely senile. But in spite of his ninety-two years, he seems physically indestructible. He is unable to express himself with any coherence except in the simplest phrases. He is excluded from the kitchen, his former domain, which puzzles and sometimes angers him. He can spend ten minutes endlessly drumming on the door with both fists before someone answers, only to tell him that he must now go away. Then he appears puzzled but satisfied, like a child who has worked through a tantrum. The simple reason for this total ban is that Christopher is now a compulsive eater. He forages for food like a jackdaw, poking around in the pantry hatch where bread and biscuits are sometimes returned. In spite of this preoccupation, he remains as wiry as fifty years ago, when he was a fighting man, driving his tank in pursuit of the retreating German army.

The problems of Christopher's deterioration are borne patiently by the community; every old man is a reminder of things to come. Earlier, when his condition was not so defined, he took to wandering off outside the monastery. One time, he was picked up several miles away by a neighbour late at night. Following this escapade, elaborate defences have been devised to keep him within a defined territory – hence the screen and door that separates the brothers' quarters and the main cloister which the community open on their way to church with their *passe-partout*. And at night, the bottom of the stairs leading to the brothers' dormitory is secured by a similar safety door. Several times, when taking my shower at 6.30 in the morning, I have heard Christopher performing his ritual of banging on the rear door of the kitchen. His energy and determination appear indomitable.

Christopher wears his habit over a pair of blue-striped pyjamas that peep out around his collar. His blue apron that he would have worn all those years when he worked in the kitchen is still tied each day around his middle. And, make no mistake, the hero is still present. With the gentle help of his nurse and minder Paul, Brother Christopher still rises each midnight to attend Night Office. At Mass each morning, he sits in his special place just next to the Prior. For the rest of the day, he wanders free for long periods. I have seen him gathering flowers like a child in the garth before the church and again in the guest garden. He is liable to pop up when least expected, as a reminder of his determination to continue his life as a monk. Vespers was ending one day when there was a scuffling sound coming from within the sacristy at the far end of the church. Presently Christopher emerged clutching a large bunch of tulips which were held out directly in front of him like a poker. He wandered across the front of the altar and left by the main door as if intent upon some business.

Another time I came across him outside the back door of the kitchen beside the herb garden. When I greeted him, he replied: 'Just a minute, it won't take long, I show you . . .' So we went for a walk. He took me to the greenhouse beside the green steel gates that lead to the outside world. He showed me the vine with its multiple bunches of tart green grapes promising an autumn harvest; we walked arm in arm around the guest garden where the previous day I had seen him happily garnering a simple bouquet of wild flowers. Now and again we fell to chattering of nothing at all. I felt he was somehow pleased to have a strange, new companion but not convinced he knew the difference between me and his own lost inner world.

Christopher is a marvellous foil to the solemnities of monastic prayer, reminding everyone now and then of their own frailty. On two or three occasions, he got up in the middle of Mass and was led off to the lavatory. Paul rises patiently on these occasions and gathers him up like a five year old. Once it occurred just at Communion time when the monks were preparing to leave their stalls and form a semi-circle standing before the altar. Paul and Christopher disappeared in a distracting clatter. But it was clear to everyone that we would slow things down until their return so that both could be houselled with the bread and wine.

There was a green bucket on the window ledge of the cloister just by the foot of the brothers' stairs. I used to look at it with some irritation and wonder why no one saw fit to put it away. One night as I made my way to Matins, there was Paul helping Christopher relieve himself; I got a cheery salute as I passed them, both concentrating on their business. The green bucket was Christopher's last chance before his two-hour vigil in the church.

The day before I came away was the feast of St Benedict, the father of Western monasticism. I turned a corner and there was Christopher, hovering predictably outside the kitchen. I went up to him and gave him a hug and wished him a happy feastday. I was suddenly aware of this iron man's body, unyielding rock beneath his monk's habit. Now suddenly we were talking; and I could actually understand a good deal of what he said.

Christopher told me that he would serve Christ to the end – 'to the end', he repeated. 'I have been here a hundred years,' he insisted. I said I believed him, that it must feel like that. Now a great smattering of Polish. And back to English. It was still a great jumble. But I fancied that he was happy in his own world, where somehow he still had his own bearings. Life might have been pared down to almost nothing, yet it seemed possible that Christopher was still in his familiar driving seat making his way home.

*

So far, the only choir monk I had met to talk to was the Prior. But, as the fox insisted when he first met the Little Prince, there is meeting and meeting.

One of my first impressions when singing the Office was how ragged it was. The Carthusian chant, I had read, is earthy and held by some to be the most prayerful of all traditions, even more than the Benedictines of Solesmes, who take great pains with their accurate and mellifluous plainsong. At Parkminster, shortage of numbers has led to reliance on individual cantors taking the lead, while the mainstream play second fiddle. I became aware immediately that the cantor leading the side opposite had a penetrating, nasal voice and, moreover, frequently kept his own peculiar timing. I was pleased to be sat next to Ignace, a giant with a good voice, who appeared musically literate. It seemed nothing short of heroic, therefore, when Ignace repeatedly fell silent and came into line with the questionable lead offered from across the floor. In my ignorance, I had not begun to understand the monastic ways.

The cantor was Dom Aloysius, a Swiss monk in his seventies. I later heard Ignace declare how fortunate he was to have Dom Aloysius as a model choir monk to look up to. And slowly I began to take notice, as I met him myself.

In Dom Aloysius, I began to perceive what I was to find in others again and again: the sight of a man faithfully performing his chosen duties in modest, loving manner. Sometimes, Aloysius would make a mistake – intone the wrong psalm or begin to read in a false place: he would cry aloud – 'Oh, no!' and begin again. In spite of his forty-plus years in England, Aloysius still guards a guttural German-Swiss accent; like many of the community, you have to concentrate hard to catch his every meaning. Each night at Lauds, he would sum up our prayers with a quotation from St Paul: 'I press on to the finish line . . .'

Pressing on to the finishing line (to correct the American translation) would serve as a summary of the man. He is small and shrunken and looks all his seventy-one years. You would perhaps pass him by in the street, choosing not to get involved with this least significant of men. But look at his face, lively and acutely tuned. Observe how energetically he performs his duties. Witness him saying Mass for the community. Above all, receive the Bread from his hands: have him say to you: 'The Body of Christ' and you suddenly know that this man has left himself for another. By means of that simple leap of faith into Christ's arms, all his foolishness is enfolded.

Singing on the opposite side of choir to Dom Aloysius is Dom Bogdan from Poland. A secular priest working in Warsaw, he came to Parkminster less than two years ago and has still to be professed. Nonetheless he already appears every inch the monk.

I was working in the kitchen one afternoon under the benign, all-seeing eye of Benedict; my task, to prepare salads for supper. I sought to express my personality and send some caring signal to these hidden monks with whom I would never converse. I halved the tomatoes (the first of the season, newly gathered in that day) in a fancy, 'dragon's teeth' fashion and mixed a dressing with vegetable oil to accompany the lettuce. My task completed, I reported back to Benedict, only to discover that I had miscounted the numbers. We were three short, and I had run out of lettuce, which had come from Bogdan's garden. I was told to go to the cloister, ring his bell and ask for a top-up supply.

This was too good to be true: a legitimate excuse to visit a choir monk's cell! It was off-side territory I had not reckoned on seeing. I headed off for Cell G (the cells at Parkminster are each designated by a letter of the alphabet). Clutching a kitchen knife, I entered the cloister. Fully 200 yards in length, its Bath-stone arches seem to go on forever. I tried to gather my thoughts as I spelt my way down the alphabet until I came to Bogdan's door. I read the Latin inscription above my head: *Qui perseveravit usque in finem, hic salvus erit* ('The man who stands firm to the end, he will be saved'). Bogdan seemed aptly to fit the formidable label: thirty years of solid Polish manhood standing six foot one and broad across the shoulder, he radiated a compact and muscular asceticism. I admired his readings from the lectern in a deep and guttural English, sculpted with difficulty by an unwilling Polish tongue.

I remembered reading in the Constitutions that when visiting a monk's cell, the caller should offer a suitable Christian greeting. I rehearsed the once-familiar '*Laudetur Jesus Christus*' that we had used as Jesuits.

71

I drew breath and pulled the bell and listened for reaction as it tinkled far away inside the cell. Presently the door opened with a sudden flourish and I mumbled my Latin tag. It must have been my slipshod English pronunciation: Bogdan's face moved not a muscle. So I plunged on, covering my pious confusion with rigmarole about being short of lettuces, my fault, lost count . . . I waved my knife at him, hoping to strengthen my cause.

Still seemingly impassive, Bogdan opened the door wider to signal me inside. He closed the door behind me and in utter surprise I took in at a glance the simple beauty of his hermitage.

We were in the ambulacrum or entrance hall running forty-six feet in length. (Surprisingly, this entrance is upstairs, an effect of the considerable ground slope on the southside of the cloister.) My eye was held by the most exquisite dried bough arrangement that graced a miniature statue of Saint Hugh with his swan standing faithfully to heel, his neck arched affectionately around his calf. Against the white-washed cell wall each leaf, an attractive nutmeg colour, appeared to stand in startling formation against its peers. I marvelled at the apparent careless ease of such fine beauty and wondered how exactly it was done. But the rule was, I could only speak about my lettuce.

'There they are,' declared Bogdan, indicating the lie of his garden down below through an open, sunlit window. I glanced past him to see row upon row of sentinel onions, planted with all the military precision of troops on parade. To one side along the path were two rows of lettuce, which had already in part been harvested.

He led me down the stairs to the ground floor. Once more my eyes were taken to an object of arresting beauty. Two rough branches lashed together with blue agricultural rope were suspended from the handrail into the stairwell to provide a primitive trapese. I imagined Bogdan's bulk, stretching and heaving early each morning upon this simple exercise machine.

We turned through his workroom and into the garden. He

stood back and indicated the lettuce row. I made along it and stooped down, knife in hand. Now at length he spoke.

'The soil is very bad.' He reached down for a handful, which he let fall through his fingers with some disdain. 'I took fifty buckets of stones before I planted anything. It needs much food. But I try.'

I located four lettuce of modest size; I felt I was picking them too soon, before they had reached full growth.

'Will you tell the kitchen that I will send the last tomorrow? Then they are finished.'

He signalled me ahead of him and, clutching my harvest, I climbed the stairs once more. Around me, the cell glowed its own vital presence. I felt that this was no prison but a humming, warm hive of energy, vitality and peace. Simple and spare it may be, yet its occupant was clearly a man of artistic taste and sensitivity. Once again I admired the dazzling display that celebrated Hugh, the founder of the English Carthusians. I turned the corner and plunged on. There came a 'Psst!' from behind: I had been heading for his Ave Maria and inner cell. I shrugged my apology and turned towards the cell door.

I turned to thank him, and he offered me for the first time a great and generous smile. The door closed on Bogdan from far-away Poland.

VI

Finding God

Finding God in all things.
St Ignatius, The Exercises

'IT has taken me all this time to realize that I'm a Jock.' I was
speaking to Dave who lost a leg at the age of fifteen. He had
just rolled up his right trouser to the knee and proudly
displayed his £8,000 worth of technology that serves him for a
replacement limb. 'I hate doing this,' was his only apology; it
helped me to hold my gaze on this complex contraption
sprouting from his kneecap. Dave is twenty-six; he used to be
a company lawyer: now he is a gold medalist in the 100 and
200 metres in the World Paralympic Games.

After ten years and despite his crippling setback, Dave has
learned to run with his talents. The athlete's physical urge he
was born with compels him to devote his energies and priori-
ties to perfecting his skills and maximizing their expression. It
is the same with the contemplative. He has caught a glimpse
of his God. Or rather, God has touched the raw marrow of his
being. Nothing further matters save the pursuit of this unique
goal. As Father Cyril puts it, everyone at Parkminster has one
thing in common: they are 'God-struck'. 'The only possible
sense of their life is to seek him who has found them. A thirst
for what is enduring and absolutely essential is born.'

One account of becoming God-struck is given by Simon,
who has just come to Parkminster. His story may not be
typical (indeed, there is no obvious archetype), but it bears all
the hallmarks of vocation, being singled out from the crowd

for no apparent reason or intrinsic merit – sometimes almost against the grain. One Monday, as we walked together, he spoke freely about his journey.

His father is Norwegian and his mother comes from England, where he was brought up. He has an older sister. Schooling was unremarkable; Simon fell short of becoming an obvious university candidate, but he was nonetheless intelligent and receptive. At the same time, he was always something of a loner. Leaving school, he drifted in and out of jobs, not finding any convincing role. Aged twenty, he met a wonderful girl, half Jamaican. It was clearly a big moment in his life so far. But all he can say now with feeling is: 'It didn't work out. It was never going to work out.'

The next fifteen years he spent as a virtual recluse, in his words, 'on the fringes of society'. He picked up seasonal jobs on the land, he didn't starve, yet at the same time, he was going nowhere. Or was he?

'My father has a log cabin high up in the northern wilds of Norway. I would spend the summers there, more or less living off the land, doing the occasional job. I love fishing. It was great. But I wasn't playing around: I wanted to know, to find out the truth. If you read the book of nature, I thought, that cannot deceive. It must always tell the truth.'

He would winter in the south of France, where his married sister lives. Here too he would find part-time jobs to keep him in bread – and still he lived on the fringes.

Then he began to read the Gospels. Over a period of some three months, he steadily developed a strong interior prayer life. 'I suddenly found a personal heart at the centre of the Universe. My book of nature had not lied.' He was now thirty-five years old, without wife, without home, with few friends. It was time to find himself a church. With darling naïveté he simply knocked on doors and inquired as to the menu within: Quaker, Methodist, Anglican. He settled for Roman Catholic and came at length to the Discalced Carmelites in Kensington, who received him into the Church. He lived with the community for the next two years as a lay member of their Third Order.

He began to write a book about his spiritual journey and became absorbed in the task. He sent his manuscript to more than one publisher. All were interested, yet none could quite place it on their list. He is now secretly relieved, judging his outpouring to have been jejeune and ill-written.

After a while, Simon grew restless. He wanted more solitude; he had looked at the Carmelites' way of life and yearned for something stricter. The Carthusians were named; he asked more questions. Aged thirty-seven, but looking ten years younger, he arrived at Parkminster.

'I have been a Catholic less than three years. I know no Latin; but I know I must become a choir monk. This is all I've ever wanted.'

We cannot tell if Simon will stay: the important thing is that he has come. His quest has been answered by a summons. He is now spending six months as a 'visiting member' in a Benedictine community, where he is learning Latin.

The quest that drew Simon for almost twenty years is age old and there are many routes, as many as those who set out. But the goal is the same for each journeyman; consequently, the means of approaching it are identical. Every man seeking God must first lose himself and, putting on Christ, he will begin his journey to the Father. The journey is a process that takes a lifetime. Nothing less is possible: for the human spirit is capable of infinite growth compared with the perfection of its Father Creator. Disappointing though it may be for the Carthusian novice, no miracle happens as he puts his head into the cowl and enters his hermitage for the first time. Like every journey, it is painful, tiring and hard work. The monk's life is an advance into the very throat of existence, where there is all is to play for. But every journey also has its watering holes and resting places, a sudden joyful view of the way ahead or perhaps a perception of the distance we have already come; a first glimpse of the sea or encounters on the way.

Man is born alone and alone he dies. In between these two fixed milestones, he must decide what is the meaning of life; and we all answer differently. The response of the contemplative is nothing if not decisive. Man will only finally encounter

God face to face in death, when each breathes forth his all to the Father who has given him life. The Carthusian solitude resembles the desert into which the Israelites were led by God. They had to leave their all and travel through the desert in search of the God of Abraham. So too the monk's given task is to meet God continually every moment of his day and night within the space of his creative solitude, which he constructs actively by his singular ability to be alone, listening to the Spirit.

The contemplative has developed the desire and capability of being alone, his own man in his own space and solitude. Viewed in this light, the hermitage is an intensely positive place where the monk is no longer seen as a walled-up fugitive so much as an artist creating an immense window opening up to the one reality that matters to man, his God who made and redeemed him. This is the holy ground that Moses found in the desert wilderness. Here he will wrestle with the angel until he finds prayer real. But in order to approach an understanding of this process, we must first look at the nature of Christian prayer.

'When you pray,' Christ advised, 'go into your chamber secretly.' Discover the space that is your own, and in this potent, creative space the encounter between God and man will steadily unfold.

We mistake the nature of our intercourse with God when we imagine that it might happen like some telephone conversation. So crude a metaphor breaks down at once. For prayer, if it is to be anything, is God's intercourse with us. Childish fantasies of imitating St Paul's encounter with Christ and all those stories of saintly visions must be set aside for good. The reality of prayer is very simple: its bedrock is man's awareness that he is a creature in the everlasting hands of God, his Maker. So it is at this point that I have to remind myself who I am and, far more importantly, who God is.

Of myself, I am a 'no-thing', a creature invited into being by my Creator. Life itself was not of my choosing, except in retrospect: my existence was the Father's initiative alone. By contrast and distinct from all things made, he is the unique being of pure existence. God names himself to Moses as the Being who holds himself in Being. 'Jahweh: I am who I am.' So that the congress between myself and God is about as comic as an ant falling in love with a whale; and one need hardly add that God is no whale.

God's immensity compared to our poverty of being is best experienced by looking up into the starry night. I never miss an opportunity to take a good, long, lingering look. To see the multitude of tiny specks of light against the dark expanse of night; I can barely believe that each twinkling pinhead is anything from ten to a thousand times the size of planet earth and light years away. And if I were to spend all night long naming and counting these myriad immense entities I would scarce have begun the task as dawn breaks; and this is only the beginning and behind this visible wealth of immeasurable organization, there lies countless more aery entities which my eye cannot even begin to descry.

God made this and keeps it in being. And we try to talk to God in our prayers: 'What is man that you should know him?' mouths the psalmist in wonderment.

Yet we know from revelation and the work of Christ, that God not only flung himself into the centre of our world as its architect, builder and model, but he has made man the chief objective of his love. In the loving work of the Trinity, God reveals himself as Maker and Re-maker: the act of creation is followed through by a second dynamic that involves our intimate and continual collaboration. The Christian life witnesses Christ born to each man afresh as human life unfolds in a continual collaboration with God's healing action. This is the central mystery that detains the Carthusian in his cell all his life long.

No words encapsulate this theme better than those of Julian of Norwich as she 'beheld the workings of the Trinity':

> God, the blissful Trinity, is everlasting Being; not only is he without beginning and without end, but equally it was always his mind to make mankind. Yet man's fair nature he first made for his own Son, the second

Person. Then when the chosen time came, with equal assent of the Trinity, he made all men at one and the same time. And in our making, he bound and oned us to himself. And in this bond we are kept as clean and noble as at the time of our making. And it is because of this precious bond that we love our Maker and like him, praise him and thank him with a joy in him that has no end. This then is the task which he works continually in every soul that shall be saved all according to this eternal plan.

This first striking statement is Julian's assertion of the priority of man's kind with regard to the Son: 'Which fair kind was first prepared for his own Son, the second Person.' In this bold, bald sentence, Julian contrives to sum up God's project of the Incarnation, not as some rescue operation put in train as a result of Adam's fall from grace and man's sin. Rather, she declares that from the first the Son was chosen to be Son of Man, the firstborn *before* Adam. This is no trick of time that views history through the wrong end of the telescope: rather, Julian offers us the privilege of God's viewpoint, who eternally decreed and agreed that God would become Man in order to effect the Divine plan of creation and elevation of our nature, so that we could be enabled to join as familiars the Divine life of the Trinity.

*

More diligent than other monks or hermits, the Carthusian 'keeps his cell'. Day by day he creates his own unique space, an environment, a culture that enables his encounter with God in prayer and the finely tuned balance of spiritual and physical routines that builds each passing day. Yet it is vital that the monastic life as a community impinges upon what is happening in cell; or there is the risk of raising a group of self-centred eccentrics living out their private fantasies of perfection. The shared community routine of public acts such as the great Night Office and most especially the community mass each morning both support and sing counterpoint to the solitary journey of the choir monk as an individual. In spite of the major time spent alone in cell, there is a vivid sense of the community collaborating and contributing as the daily life of the monastery unfolds.

At three in the afternoon on St Bruno's eve, the church was the scene of much quietly contained activity. Dom Aloysius (at the age of seventy-one) was to be seen scaling the altar like a mountain kid in order to place his flower arrangements on the topmost pinnacle. Bogdan was busy in the sacristy mending the floor and putting up a shelf; while a group of readers and cantors were rehearsing the complexities of the forthcoming Night Office.

More mundanely each day, the community shares a common timetable set out for all to follow: when the bell for the Angelus rings, each monk will be saying the same prayer, lunch is taken at the common hour; the community at large is called from the cloister hermitages, the garden or kitchen by the bell that summons them to matins, Mass or evening prayers: now each individual finds himself part of the one praying community in church. Most important is the shared morning Eucharist that inaugurates and informs each day. The creative tension between the pull of the community living and praying together and the individual hermit fashioning his own solitary way is the secret to the Carthusian dynamic. His activity – God-watching – lies at the heart of the contemplative way. The Carthusian essays to enter the love life of the Trinity as Father, Son and Holy Spirit contemplate and continually facilitate that work of their hands, the world they create, redeem, and are even now shaping.

I deliberate in the present tense because we need to break out of the concept of the world as some kind of ancient stage set, designed by a skilful agent, long since departed. Our only valid experience of the world continues to be that it is utterly fresh, as if at every moment we see and experience it for the first time. In this way we are invited to explore and live its deeper mystery, the mystery of a dawn that God awakens in us every moment of our being. By accepting this eternal 'now-moment' of creation offered continually in our experience of change, we open ourselves to the intimate dynamic of the Trinity – God with his hands in the dough, God making the bread of his creation in order to feed us his loving purpose of renewal.

A child has this direct contact with the vibrant world all around it; he cannot fail to be overwhelmed at all the sensory wealth that presses in from every side. As we 'mature', we can so easily grow numb and lose contact. My friend Sam, aged five, came across from Canada with his parents and young brother Dominic to visit Gran and Grandad. Stepping into a great aeroplane, arriving in a strange new land, taking the train all the way to Somerset – this must have been exciting stuff for a five-year-old lad. But when he saw Gran's pegs on the washing line in the back garden, he just said: 'Wow!'

Gran's pegs are red. So 'Wow!' Sam still has the wonder of now.

*

Wonder infuses the Carthusian's journey. He has travelled far to reach this still, silent hermitage; within its confines, he will travel limitless miles more. And his lifelong companion in his journey is Mary, Christ's mother. Chief among saints, Mary is both his example and his enabler; and critically – for the celibate monk – she is Woman. Any man who closes himself to the benign influence of the feminine is at risk; the celibate is in particular danger of suffering psychic distortion by his aloneness. Allowing Mary to pervade his daily life provides the crucial corrective to his solitary bachelor life. In every hermitage, the ante-room to the inner cell contains a shrine to Our Lady and is known as the Ave Maria. Mary's life work was to mother Christ: in Hopkins' words:

> Gave God's infinity
> Dwindled to infancy
> Welcome in womb and breast
> Birth, milk, and all the rest

I myself have had lifelong difficulties in finding the cult of Our Lady meaningful. For years I have kept her at arm's length, bringing forward all the old familiar objections. I prefer to access my God direct, I have no time for miracles and spinning suns in the sky, Mariology is an invention of the Church to satisfy the mass market, the rosary is a repetitive prayer made popular in mediaeval times when common folk could not read.

When I was ten and my sister twelve, we were crouching under the protection of a Morrison shelter (a cumbersome steel table with mesh sides erected by a caring wartime Government in our sitting room) while a doodlebug blasted through the house with terrifying force and noisome evil. Our parents were still coming downstairs carrying our baby sister in her crib as the front door blew in. In that encapsulated moment of terror, I remember my surprise at my sister piping up the Hail Mary. As an afterthought, I joined in. My sister had the presence of mind – and heart – to cry out to her namesake, Mary.

Mary's own Yes, her Fiat on learning God's plan for her, made her in that instant his mother. Yet it took her entire life of prayer and patient faith to understand it to the full. In Luke's Gospel, after the distressing account of the young Jesus missing for three days and then being found in the Temple, Luke offers barely a glimpse of Mary's mind: 'his mother stored up all these things in her heart'. Yet it suffices. Mary sets an example that we all have to follow. Far from setting her apart from us, her Divine Motherhood offers us the perfect example of how we too must approach God, or rather permit him to overwhelm us. For he is asking of us the self-same surrender to his purpose in the exact words used when the angel appeared to Mary. True, we are not to become the unique mother of God. Yet he seeks something very similar: he asks me to let him in so that he can mother me.

Mary continued throughout her life to respond to God's meaning – we see her at the edge of the crowds that in their urgent need press constantly in around her Son; at the foot of the cross when most other friends had fled; in the upper room after the Ascension, where she 'joined in continuous prayer' with the small and frightened huddle that was the fragile embryo of the Church. Thirty years before she had opened her womb to the Holy Spirit and accepted the pregnancy that was Jesus. Now she witnesses and participates once more in the collective fiat to the Spirit at Pentecost, when the Church as a new community opens itself to the might of God's plan in its midst.

Each Christian soul is not only feminine in respect of receiving God's Spirit, but virginal too. And we remain virgins to God's invitation at every moment of our life, right up to the moment of our death. In her book *An Image Darkly Forming*, a fascinating psychological case study, Bani Shorter reinvests the word 'virgin' with its primitive meaning. Far from being one who shies from men or is for the time being untouched, she writes that the virgin is continually open and ready for impregnation. In the myth of Persephone, the daughter of Demeter is dragged away to the underworld of Hades against her will. Here she is initiated and bears a child. The Attic Greek *kore* means simply a young girl of marriageable age and is the equivalent of *parthenos* or in Hebrew *almah*, both words used of Mary in the Gospels.

The early huddle of Christians hiding in a secret room after the disaster of Christ's catastrophic death were soon to know the might of the Spirit at Pentecost: they in turn had to say their yes, give their *fiat* of cooperation that was to continue throughout their lives ahead.

This calling to be open to the Spirit of God is lifelong and at every moment of each day. Hopkins booms it forth in his opening stanza of *The Wreck of the Deutschland*:

> Thou mastering me
> God! giver of breath and bread;
> World's strand, sway of the sea;
> Lord of living and dead;
> Thou hast bound bones and veins in me, fastened me flesh,
> And after it almost unmade, what with dread,
> Thy doing: and dost thou touch me afresh?
> Over again I feel thy finger and find thee.

VII

PARKMINSTER, THE PLANT

Foxes have holes and the birds of the air
have nests, but the Son of Man has
nowhere to lay his head.
Matthew 8:20

THE French Carthusians of La Grande Chartreuse, as we have seen, came to Sussex almost by stealth. Their subterfuge in signing a contract of sale dressed in layman's clothes and resurrecting for the purpose a noble handle seems at best underhand, at worst devious. Yet, in the mid-nineteenth century, there was a very real anti-Roman sentiment on both sides of La Manche. England of the 1870s – and still more France – were countries in which a Roman cleric, and especially a monk, must move with the utmost caution.

The French Carthusians, in company with every other Religious Order in France, were once more making contingency plans for moving their communities away from the impending storm of anti-religious legislation against a rising background of intimidation at home and suspicion abroad. (They had learned their lesson during the Revolution that to allow the storm to make its own way to their door lost them the initiative.) Crossing the Channel, they found a land of known Protestant affiliation where the Catholic establishment was still tenuous. The Roman Catholic hierarchy had indeed been permitted to resettle only twenty years previously, but the manner of its restoration turned out to be thoroughly alarming. In 1848, Bishop Nicholas Wiseman had proved himself a successful diplomatic envoy from Pius IX to Palmerston, Victoria's prime minister, in re-establishing after three hundred troubled years formal state recognition of the ancient Faith. But two years later, the newly promoted Cardinal Archbishop of Westminster chose to issue his first pastoral letter to English Catholics grandly entitled 'From without the Flaminian Gate' (the ancient Roman gate that looks north towards England). In his own mind, Wiseman was joyfully announcing his new-won spiritual jurisdiction over English Roman Catholics: yet his curious territorial delineations sounded to ordinary English ears like a declaration of war. Above the hue and cry that it provoked on every side rose Victoria's own querulous complaint: 'Am I no longer to be queen in my own lands?'

Having struck this needlessly triumphant note at the outset of his return to England, Cardinal Wiseman had to work long and hard allaying fears that Catholic Emancipation meant a renewal of foreign intervention in England's domestic affairs. These preoccupations apart, he was cool towards religious orders; memories of bitter divisions during the long missionary period since the Reformation, when Jesuits seemed set against secular priests and vice-versa, were still vivid. The sudden arrival of a party of French hermits seemed to him a distraction, as unwanted as it was ill-timed. On two occasions, the advance party led by Dom Pascal Sené attempted a meeting with the Cardinal. Both times he was reported to be 'away'. In the meantime, Dom Pascal had been pleased to receive the patronage of their new ordinary, Bishop Grant of Southwark, whose manner towards the newcomers was by contrast both warm and enabling. (He was later to make it clear that his was an impoverished diocese in constant need of capital, a commodity he believed was not in short supply with the new arrivals. His suggestion was met generously and without further demur.) As the handful of monks settled into their new home at Parknowle, the bishop encouraged them in their religious observances. They could not yet achieve canonical status, which would allow them to set up a formal cloister, but already the Blessed Sacrament was reserved, and he insisted that they wear their habits and practise their rule. 'Yes, yes!! you must,' he wrote familiarly in reply to their inquiry as to whether they should already be living their full monastic routine, 'it's the way you have to live.' For the next six years a swelling community was to fit into the former Boxall establishment and oversee the vast building site on its doorstep while attempting to maintain their tranquil timetable as Carthusians. As the buildings neared completion, some twenty monks were living in community – and attempting some kind of cell solitude – still in the original mansion. It took some doing within the confines of a house intended as no more than a modest gentleman's country home.

*

At La Grande Chartreuse, Dom Charles Marie was proving to be an energetic and expansive General Superior. So far he had initiated the building of five new monasteries in six years; but Parkminster was to be something special. It was destined to play a key role in the elaborate game plan to provide for the possible future evacuation of the numerous Carthusian communities on the Continent now living under imminent threat of expulsion.

Dom Pascal was formally appointed Rector of Parknowle by the Reverend Father, taking at the same time the patronage of St Hugh, the first English Carthusian. In a fulsome letter to his General Superior written in Latin, he looks forward to them gathering together, as a new family of monks zealous in their practice of the Carthusian Statutes. Yet almost at once comes the news that he is to be replaced by an Irishman, Dom Hugh McMahon, one of the first advance party. What had gone wrong?

Buying the new property had been safely negotiated with a vendor who at any time might possibly have become hostile, but then of a sudden came difficulties in obtaining the vital canonical status from the local hierarchy. As soon as he was aware of this setback, Dom Pascal hastened to London, where he was met by a foot-shuffling Bishop Grant: there were one or two snags ... It was not clear how they had arisen. To be frank, one or two provisos must be met. The bishop went on to detail them: (1) There could be only twelve religious in the new foundation. (2) They must lead a regular life.

(3) The enclosure had to come directly under the Holy See.

The first of these conditions meant that the whole purpose behind the master evacuation plan, potentially involving the rehousing of scores of monks from more than one monastery, was ruled out. And the third condition (one could humbly overlook the slur contained in the second) sent an instant frisson of impermanence upon the concept of re-establishing a Carthusian foundation in England.

The very scale of their plans for England was now in jeopardy, especially after Reverend Father had received confirmation directly from Rome along similar lines. It was understood that behind the scenes the Cardinal was incensed that a group of powerful French monks, rich from the profits of their sales of alcohol, were planning to invade his domain. It was no secret that Wiseman had been a lifelong teetotaller.

But the Carthusians were not ones to give up lightly. As a first move to counter feelings that the foundation was an exclusively French affair, appointing an Irishman as superior seemed prudent. (Coincidentally, the Cardinal had been brought up at Waterford from the age of three.) It was next discovered that where Rome had already sanctioned a foundation, as they had done in this instance, it could not be abandoned. Unofficial word soon came through from Rome that the Carthusians should quietly go ahead with the original building plans for their monastery.

The site, which had been acquired in 1873, had been purchased by them precisely because it was 'green field'. The original Parknowle would be retained (in its present diminished state, it is now the guesthouse), while the new buildings would be laid out adjacent on a slightly sloping site that required the whole monastery to be swung round a few degrees to the north.

Given the size of the venture, these plans were accordingly put in hand on a major scale that was already familiar in Victorian Britain, where the entire canal system was now being rapidly superseded by the railways. Such upheaval was quite unknown in the calm backwaters of inland Sussex. Parkminster, as it was now known, was to be something utterly extraordinary, a double-sized monastery capable of housing two entire communities should the need arise. First plans had already been drawn up by Normand et Fils of Calais, who had recently completed the monastery of Montreuil in Provence to the satisfaction of their client. Sending these plans to England, Dom Charles Marie noted that while they might appear somewhat grand – as many as forty cells were projected – it was important to meet with English expectations (*'l'esprit Anglais l'exige'*: a striking sepia shot of how at that time one nation viewed the other). The resultant local upheaval proved considerable. Roads were widened and diverted so as to obtain good site access; cottages were built for labourers and as work got under way in earnest, a resident policeman was posted to keep order among a workforce that would eventually swell to 700 men.

A brickworks was opened to the north of the site where, it was noted, there was ample good clay. Four kilns were erected to achieve a manufacturing capacity of as many as 60,000 bricks per fortnight. It was an output that needed to be sustained, since an estimated six million bricks would be used in the entire project. The large quantities of coal needed to fuel these kilns were brought in by train to Partridge Green, then carted along leafy Sussex lanes in great wagons. In addition, large quantities of Bath stone were procured and brought in by barge as far as Henfield quay. Nearer to hand at Slinfold, a quarry was opened to yield a grey stone that, part-dressed, would be used extensively for all exterior walls. A harder, almost white stone from Swanage was used for all the window surrounds. To accommodate this industry, a chantier or yard was set up where the stone could be dressed by skilled masons. It also housed a large joinery works that turned out all sash windows, doors and other such necessities. Yet the entire church furniture of wood, panelling and choir stalls in French oak, presently to be installed in the church would come from France, where the client already had good experience of existing craftsmen's skills.

Other Continental imports included paving stones for the cloisters – magnificent black Belgian marble, and slow-growing spruce from Archangel, to make up the roof beams and trusses that would be the skeletal construction for the massive church tower. So the complex work continued.

In the spring of 1876, a solemn celebration was held to dedicate the work in hand and bless the foundation stone of the church. Its purpose was both an exercise in good will, even publicity, and an act of spiritual dedication. The guest list was as ambitious as could be conceived, comprising a broad sweep of local and national notables. The mixed response must have been discouraging.

The Duke of Norfolk was at his daughter-in-law's funeral; Lady Fullerton was prevented by ill-health. If it sounded simply like the parable of the wedding feast, all might have been understood; but there was an unmistakable feeling of mistrust and suspicion about the scale of the works and who was achieving them – and to what purpose? it was asked.

Nothing daunted, and with another parable in mind that would have them in from the highways and the byways come what may, a large marquee was erected to cover the future area of the church. Coats of arms of the twelve former charterhouses once scattered around the British Isles were curiously fashioned in zinc and displayed theatrically around the tent in heraldic boast. It was all a trifle unseemly. And overnight a high wind brought this ambitious erection to the ground, only for it to be patiently restored at dawn for the day of dedication. The ceremonies lasted two hours. To the participating monks, this was nothing. What did seem hard was the practicality that they had been persuaded to enter in procession carrying flowers. The Annals are clear on this detail: it hurt.

Alongside the great marquee, a second tent had been put up; and here the 170 guest eventually sat down to feast after the religious solemnities.

The menu read as follows:

MENU

Ris lice au beurre d'écrevisse
Brumoise à l'essence de racines
Vermicelle au pêcheur
Croquettes d'huîtres d'Ostende
Cannetons de poisson à la cardinal
Aspic de filets de soles en Bellevue
Mayonnaise de filets de carpes
Gelantine d'anguille au beurre de Montpelier
Petites bouches de homard
Salmis d'eperlans à la Provençale
Pains de poissons à la puré de champignons
Blanquette de turbot à la Béchamel
Petites caisses d'huîtres aux fines herbes
Filet de sole à la Venitienne
Truite à la Ravigote
Buissons de petits homards
Darnes d'esturgeon à la Chambord
Buissons d'ecrevisses
Gros paté dresse de saumon

Salade d'anchois – salade Italienne – Asperges à la Hollondaise
petits pois au beurre – Harricot verts liés –
pommes de terres maître d'hotel

Gelée au citron
Charlotte Russe
Gelée à la Grande Chartreuse

Fromages – la various aux abricots

Gateau Mousseline
Nougat à la Chantilly
Religeuse au moka
Chartreuses de pommes
Poires au compôtes
Gateau Nappolitain
Meringue Chantilly
Abricots à la Condé

Champagne – Hock – Hérès – Burgundy

90

Astonishing, mouth-watering to transcribe into our own day. Yet who came in from Brighton, Paris or Brightlingsea to realize such gastronomic ecstasies? What quantities of food did each individual on average consume? Were all served with the entire rolling menu? Questions I put to Raymond Blanc of *Quatre Saisons*, who confessed himself perplexed. It would take him too much time to think it all through.

In the Annals, the narrator adds his own *excusez-moi*, a gloss upon such excesses: 'As you will have guessed, this is not our cup of tea [your storyteller freely translates]: in fact, faced with this feast we sat to one side and ate our own kind of fare. We were content. Brother Benedict, however, declared that he had asked for another helping of bread, only to be ignored by attendant caterers; as a consequence he rose from table hungry.'

*

I had spent a morning with John Warren, the architect in overall charge of the extensive renovation plans currently in train at Parkminster. Funded initially by the Carthusians but now with a considerable subvention from English Heritage, the project is in three stages and will last five years.

His appointment as architect began when he was driving past Parkminster some ten years ago and on an impulse rang the doorbell. Introductions were effected and some months later the Prior telephoned to say that their incumbent architect had died: would a formal meeting be possible? This led to his taking over the onerous task of advising on fabric maintenance. Obviously, he began with a thoroughly detailed structural survey of the entire plant. Conducted over a period of three months, it ran to over sixty pages. This provided a starting-point that led on to today's three-stage plan following the decision to refurbish completely the existing buildings. But first, serious and probing questions must be asked. Were the English Carthusians content to remain locked in to a monastery designed by their forebears to meet a completely different spread of circumstances? Should a modest-sized community of twenty men continue to inhabit (and maintain) a notable group of buildings intended for three times their number? Quite simply, would Parkminster's capacity ever be fully taken up again? It would not be enough to view the monastery like some hotelier filling beds – nine cells occupied: twenty-seven to go. Entire blocks of the original buildings now lie empty and unused. The printing press was last used twenty years ago; the tailors' shop over forty years ago. Perhaps a new secular use might be found for some of these spaces that would prove neutral to the religious purpose of the remainder of the buildings. For like the Albert Memorial, which seemed such a good idea at the time, the fabric needs continual maintenance as each year passes.

After examining the cost of re-location and building a 'green field' monastery (Ireland as well as the Far East were on the agenda), it was agreed to take the line of least resistance and remain *in situ*. English Heritage were consulted and soon became whole-hearted collaborators in the restoration scheme. Although less than 150 years old, Parkminster is the only working model of a mediaeval monastery, a unique witness to 800 years of monasticism in England. For the Carthusians it was a hard decision to make. No one likes leaving home, least of all an ancestral home of over a century's standing.

'I come to the monastery most days of the week. Its buildings are full of peace and reassurance; I always go away feeling better.' John Warren sat in his wood-framed, twelfth-century Sussex farmhouse and talked about his task at Parkminster. I asked him whether it was well built, and he replied ambivalently. The materials and workmanship he could not fault. He instanced the Belgian marble, the Bath stone; again the skilled plumbers who had beaten out the lead covering on the bell tower roof: 'Perfectly even, so hard to do – and it has lasted extremely well.' But he criticized some serious mistakes in basic building techniques: timbers were received into stone walls without adequate protection against damp. And going into the cloisters, he had been saddened to see how the marble pavement was being eroded by rising damp. Further investigation revealed that the whole cloister had been laid upon a clay bed on the false assumption that this was damp proof. On the contrary, clay is slowly pervious and over the years the cloister surface has steadily deteriorated.

These clinical strictures aside, John Warren's overall enthusiasm for Parkminster endures, and he encouraged me to take time off to come to grips with some of the buildings' hidden secrets: the stained glass in the reliquary, the roof void above the church, the view from the bell-tower.

*

Feeling not a little irreligious, I spent the next day clambering over the buildings armed with a camera. Living in the community, I had absorbed the tangible peace that Parkminster's buildings radiate. It gives a totally different perspective to view the buildings objectively, as it were through the architect's eyes, who sees an extensive plant needing a continual repair and maintenance programme. For many years, there has been a minimum of exterior maintenance, which has meant a steady build-up to crisis proportions. This became apparent when the monastery was hit by the hurricane that lashed the whole of Southern England during the winter of 1987.

The storm uprooted trees, ripped open roofs and flung tiles to the ground below. Serious damage to the library roof left gaping holes through which rainwater poured; but as dawn broke, a red builder's truck appeared at the bottom of the drive. Peter Reilly and Les Holt had arrived armed with tarpaulins, ladders and roofing felt. Peter, a Glaswegian, had been a Carthusian novice for some nine months before returning to his true calling as a general builder. Assessing the extent of the storm, he had telephoned Les (our paramedic whom we met earlier) in the morning, saying, 'They'll be needing us at Parkminster.' When they arrived, they could not even negotiate the drive, due to the large number of trees tumbled across its length. But by the end of the day, the library had been secured and what was to become a full-scale renovation project lasting the next decade had unofficially begun.

The best way to view Parkminster as a whole is to ascend the bell-tower which is centred over the nave of the church.

My journey began beside the foundation stone which was laid and blessed and feasted upon in the 1880s. There is a lengthy trudge up the stone stairway of the clock tower with its repeated stained glass spyholes looking out to the cloister orchard below. At every landing, some thoughtful monk has placed a chair, where less fit brethren may gain their breath. Soon one arrives at two oak doors, side by side: the library and the reliquary chapel. On and up, turning three more flights, until at length I passed through a door into a vast loft.

This rests immediately over the roof of the library, which itself sits on top of the chapter house on the ground floor 100 feet below. Small openings in the roof are blocked off by chicken-wire to deter invading daws. In living memory, a peregrine has nested here: a huge pile of twigs that it might have gathered with its mate still lie in the centre of the loft. (Brother Benedict tells the story of suddenly being confronted by this noble bird in the cloister, where it had been lost and confined for two days. Doing his rounds with the lunches, he was startled as the hawk stooped to rest momentarily on his trolley. He rang the door bell, and with not a moment's hesitation the bird flew through into the cell to make its escape through the garden beyond.)

Making one's way out of this first loft, you gain access to the main church tower by means of a wooden walkway that takes over the route from now on. The trusses thrust and push together like great knotted limbs. Some, as much as four foot square, are bolted and braced together to lock the base of the bell-tower soaring directly above. Like some slave master on shipboard, I walk the great gantry that runs the full length of the church below. Six feet down on either side, the church roof arches its humped back, undulated like a whale's, a sooty leviathan in frozen stasis. Builders have left small piles of rubble, as if long ago they suddenly grew tired of their task and must make their homes by sunset, never to return. I come to a grating in the roof through which passes the rope of the Angelus bell: peering down, I descry the polished order of the church below, its wooden floor and pews glowing warmly in the lush sunlight pouring across the interior. As I clamber along this dusty wasteland, I feel separated and apart from the quiet spiritual process going on in the monastery below.

I take a deep breath and begin my ascent of the bell tower. The ladder soars away above me; I grip it with both hands and feel my camera bag bump across the small of my back. I have always disliked heights, ever since I fell from a crab-apple tree as a boy. At the ladder's rickety summit there is a small trap-door: it lifts aside to reveal a secret aerie. Right beside me, the massive church bell sits silent but menacing. Its name-plate still reads 'Blews of Birmingham', and I wonder if they are still in business like their bell. (Checking later, I could find no trace of them.) The platform is cramped for space but caged in with chicken-wire. I am growing increasingly wary of the great bell, hanging silent yet with all the potential of an unex-ploded bomb. I glance at the clock tower and am reassured by the time. It is 12.25: no one is due to pull the bell for three more hours. It is a cloudless September day. From my high perch I scan out across the level Sussex terrain to where the South Downs rise. At one point, their smooth yet intricate skyline is fragmented by a battered wooded remnant, all that now remains of Chanctonbury Ring. In a field two miles off, a line of bright green canvas tents: I hear the cry of boys' voices bearing down upon the wind. Scouts enjoying the freedom of summer. My eyes come back to the foreground: down below in the great orchard spreads a chaotic straggle of apple trees, lightly laden this year. The giant striding cloister hems in this green oasis and beyond are the neat roofs of the hermitages like dolls' houses in polite line. To the south, I count eleven; on the north there are only ten. I puzzle over this conundrum and realize that here they stand lengthwise rather than end on. Facing me only fifty feet away, the great church tower rises massively into the sky. I am perched just below the clock-face, perhaps 120 feet above the ground.

Behind me lies the garth dissected by the black brick pathway leading to the gatehouse. Pear and apple trees are still neatly espaliered against the cloister walls, yet box and yew have run amok and tumble in a jungle of confusion on either side of the main church entrance. On the left of the garth, the grey, gaunt facade of the obedience yard, where dozens of brothers once lived, lies empty; opposite is the kitchen yard and beyond again the dull bulk of the guesthouse.

All around the monastery wallows in sunbathed solitude, its walls steeped in silent time, while like lapping waves still come the distant cries of boys. Do they know what lies in waiting here that their distant cries assault? Would they wonder at the business of these men five or six times their age? John Warren's story comes to mind: he first visited Parkminster as a boy scout, and he returned as the master physician of its fabric.

I take my farewell by gazing up at the majestic stainless steel cross that tops the tower above me. A pair of daws circle the steeple, noisily disputing over a preferred perch of the moment. Now off and away they wheel into the deep blue sky.

I gaze down upon this vast array of buildings and remember the inventory in the Annals proudly detailing their completion after six years' long toil:

Tower	202ft. (cross 10ft)
Church	length, 157ft.; width, 28ft.
	choir panelling, 30ft; height to ceiling, 58ft.
Cloisters	South, 599ft.; North, 440ft.;
	East & West, 377ft.
	width, 9ft.8ins.; height, 14ft.11ins.
Total length	(including entrance cloisters etc.): 1,170 yards
Library	72ft.9ins. x 26ft. and 21ft. high
Chapter House	61ft. x 26ft. and 22ft. high
Prior's Hall	42ft. x 28ft.
North Obedience	length 238ft. x 21ft. width
containing:	bakery, forge, laundry, repair shops, paint shop, stables, hay barns and 11 beds
Central Obedience	32 beds
36 Cells:	56ft. x 46ft.
Total Cost	£200,000

Viewing all this from above, I am reminded of Christ being taken up by Satan to the pinnacle of the Temple. My own temptation is to question the boldness of scale with which this enormous pile was conceived. Did the French monks really believe the English required it of them? Why did they insist on building a double-sized monastery that was to last for all time? The decision lay with Reverend Père Charles Marie who, as we have seen, was something of a master builder, completing five monasteries in six years. There can hardly have been time to think!

Yet there might be another explanation. Given the uncertain political background, with its fierce hatred of all outward manifestations of religious belief, might not the Carthusians have been tempted simply to lay down the gauntlet in escaping to England, an alien and largely Protestant land? In this light, Parkminster becomes a boast and a challenge, a citadel of faith, like some Crusader fortress in the distant Holy Land.

Parkminster today remains impressive, and there is a discernible quickening as the renovation works slowly proceed. Notwithstanding its huge scale, it functions well enough as a monastery. The church is a fine, well-cared-for space; the kitchens are well appointed and designed; the cells that are used house their monks efficiently. But it is the empty two thirds that is the worry. For a brief period in all its 150 years has the monastery been fully manned. At the turn of the century, ninety-three monks lived here – sixty choir monks and thirty-three brothers. For the first time since its inception, it met the purpose it was built for, to offer safe refuge for Carthusians expelled from the Continent. The ark was full; but briefly. Within a few years the political mood shifted and the monks returned to their homelands, leaving once more an uneasy rump, a community purportedly English but whose majority of members spoke English as their second tongue. Throughout the years, Englishmen have never come to Parkminster in any numbers, prompting the present Prior to wonder whether the contemplative was ever in their temperament. Numbers have been sustained only with difficulty; yet at Parkminster today, there is a sudden quickening of vocations and numbers are rising encouragingly. As always, it is the ratio of perseverance that holds the key to a thriving community.

David Knowles notes in his massive survey of English monasticism that the Carthusians grew quite suddenly in the fifteenth century. Having established only three monasteries in their first three hundred years, within the space of less than fifty years their number rose to eight; at the very time when Wyclif and the Lollards were mounting fierce attacks on the probity of the Church. These foundations were in the main lavishly endowed by patrons who were either royal or with close connections to the monarch. Sheen in London, founded by Henry V in 1414, could house at least thirty choir monks. One can therefore point to historic precedents that are forerunners of Parkminster's size and ambition. But what has always weighed upon the spirit has been its sheer size.

*

Carefully I edge backwards down the shaky ladder whence I came. I feel above my head to secure the trapdoor, grateful that the great bell still lies mute. Presently, I can relax back on the comparative safety of the wooden gantry that leads back to the library tower and its circular stone staircase.

I next want to explore the clock-tower, at least as far as the clock-room, which is reached by a tight stone stairway within the walls overlooking the graveyard. The clock maker is M. Chavin of Grenoble, whose company must have made clocks for many a charterhouse in France. The works lie naked like a car engine ripped from its proper housing; their machinations remain a mystery to the layman. The winding mechanism sits silently apart; the main works have two drums cogged together and wound about with taut steel ropes that shoot purposefully upwards. The steady clanking process of the claw-like device chewing its cog mate is interrupted by a sudden whirring as a pair of fins go into action. There is a jerky motion and a satisfying answering response as, high above, the bells ring out the quarter.

I climb up higher to the tribune and gaze along the full length of the church to where the distant high altar stands flanked by carved panels of the four great monastic giants – Benedict, Dominic, Francis, Bruno. Below is the segregated lower half of the church where formerly the brothers came to hear the Office sung apart. Beside the great screen that divides the church, Bill the chippy patiently toils. I had spoken to him earlier that morning about his task of repairing the underfloor which had been discovered riddled with dry rot. The original design provided insufficient cross-ventilation, architect Warren explained; and there is considerable anxiety that it will be a similar story once the main church floor is lifted. Meanwhile, Bill goes ahead patiently laying fresh timbers and surveying the complex jig-saw of parquet floor that he must soon relay.

The traditional Carthusian design breaks the church into two portions of unequal size: the main nave is dedicated to choir monks while the brothers, or *conversi*, are confined to their own area, where they take part in the Offices as silent witnesses. In a similar way cathedral congregations in the past were distanced from the sacred mysteries by the great rood screen and choir.

This apartheid has now been abandoned and today the brothers sit alongside the choir monks in the main church. If they wish, they may take a full singing role in performing the Office. And whether or not they sing, every monk now takes his turn at reading the lessons.

At one o'clock, I had arranged to meet Brother Augustine. With justifiable pride he shows me his cider press, housed in what is reputed to be the largest cellar in Sussex. Lying below the kitchen are a series of cavernous arches that retreat into stygian darkness to swallow a line of black oaken casks. These are second-hand rum barrels of indeterminate age. I am invited to smell one in a row of four newcomers which are empty and still awaiting their first fill of new cider. The aroma is powerful and sweet, sustaining a strong memory of its former contents: this reek of mature rum and the oak itself slowly impart an extra tang to the maturing contents.

Standing proud in the centre of the cellar is the hydraulic press. Installed some eight years ago, it replaced a traditional manual press whose wooden-threaded screw had to be man-handled by three or four monks working a capstan. By contrast, the new press makes light of its work.

Apples arrive down a chute from the upper courtyard and are first introduced to the crusher. From here the pulp is folded in nylon netting to make so-called 'cheeses', regular squares moulded by a wooden frame to fit one on top of another under the press. Some ten to twelve are built in a tower to feed a single pressing: each cheese is separated from the next by a sheet of five-ply. When the cheeses are piled high so that they almost touch the press top, the hydraulic pump is switched on, and the apple juice gushes out. They remain under pressure for some two hours until no more juice flows. Sixty, perhaps seventy gallons result. Ordinary white granulated sugar is added, a pound to the gallon. Quantities are predetermined and a concentrated master liquid is prepared before pumping it directly into the first empty barrel. This is then filled to its brim with neat apple juice and left open for two days.

Augustine has been in charge of the cellar for nine years and speaks like an enthusiastic master brewer. He describes the thrill each year as the first pressing flows out with all its autumnal generosity.

'I like to mix the apples well: some Bramleys in each pressing to give a nice sharp taste,' he comments. But each pressing varies from the last. He reckons on producing 120 gallons a day during pressing week, when the apples are gathered in straight from the orchards. A normal annual yield will be around 700 gallons. But this year apples are scarce, and it will be hard to produce half that quantity.

In the first two days, the newly primed barrel froths and overflows onto the cellar floor below as the initial fermentation charges ahead. Then the upper bung on the top of the barrel is put in place, holding a glass airlock seal that allows the barrel to breathe out the carbon dioxide yielded by the fermentation for perhaps as long as eighteen months. Once a barrel has ceased to produce the gas, it is bung sealed and the cider is left in the wood for at least three years.

The resultant apple wine is a fine-tasting, full-bodied quaff. The samples I enjoyed at lunch each day during my stay varied from a thick, sweetish, almost mead-like amber liquid, to a thinner, straw-coloured cider with a sharp bite to the palate.

We leave the cellar and pass through the entrance cloisters around the garth and come into the Obedience yard. Resembling nothing so much as a workhouse or even a nine-teenth-century prison, the buildings rise severe and grey on both sides of a long grassy yard. Augustine demonstrates his laundry which, to my surprise, he works single-handed to give the community a weekly service. The equipment is ultra-modern and of commercial rather than domestic design, yet it still seems a remarkable achievement for one man. Augustine is also skilled in metal repairs and garage work and shows me his workshop.

At the corner of the yard we come to the printshop, which last worked some twenty years ago. Three French presses are still in place, as well as a Stanhope hand-press. Upstairs in the setting room lie numerous racks of metal type-faces sufficient for full-scale, quality book production. In the paper store, a loft to one side, are unbound sheets of the complete works of Denis the Carthusian. The quality of the work is admirable, equal to any leading private press. The library of Trinity College, Dublin, has recently bought in a set of sheets for binding. Augustine goes on to tell me how the last printer, a layman, had worked for over twenty years in the shop until he was well into his seventies. But now the machinery lies idle and unused.

Behind the printshop is the saw-mill with two pitsaws capable of planking a mature tree. We cross over to the bindery, which is one of the last craftshops still in operation. Two monks are practising the ancient skills. Again, the work-shop is well appointed: a fine oak hand-press bears its makers' brass plate, 'Foucher Frères, Paris', and leather pieces of many colours lie in piles beside several attractive examples of work in hand.

We emerge into the afternoon sun. The great drive through the centre of the courtyard leads to double doors opening into the cloister orchard. It is not hard to imagine the old days when a pair of shires would have drawn their cartloads of apples out across the yard and round to the cellar chute on just such an afternoon. Or again, one might almost hear the saw-mill sing as the phut-phutting steam engine sends its power along the belt-drive that makes the fly-wheel spin and causes the blade to scream as it bites the full length of a bole.

It is 1.15. The Angelus sounds out. All work ceases as every monk gathers himself to reflect once more on the eternal mystery of God's commerce with Man. Time stands still. My reverie is over.

I thank Augustine for his time. Tomorrow I leave for home, so we make our farewells. We embrace like brothers; the kiss of peace is a warm, human hug that sums up all our genuine affection and commitment to each other. I will pray for him daily and remember him always, as I will each of the other brothers I have lived with at Parkminster. From now on, I am part of their lifelong family.

VIII

THE EUCHARIST

Esto nobis praegustatum,
Mortis in examine.

FIRST Communion. The nuns prepared us well. When the
day came, my sister wore white and had a veil pinned to her
hair, while we boys were all issued with unfamiliar white
brocade armbands, a double fold hanging down all etched in
gold. My mother fastened this onto my left arm just above my
elbow, carefully doing up the two 'hooks and eyes' which I
thought more appropriate to a girl's bodice. And, of course,
we had all gone to the priest the day before to make our First
Confession: 'I have teased my sister. I have been disobedient
to my parents . . .'

We were not given wine. That was not to come on the liturgical menu until much later. We were merely told in hushed
tones that Jesus was coming to us. The nuns did their best.

The mystery of the Eucharist, the Christian's food for his
journey through life, is so powerful as to overwhelm with its
meaning. And yet, as Cyril would say, it's very simple.

Bread and wine, the plainest, most common food known to
men. What we set before friends, bring home to our wife and
children, what makes us glad and brings us together around
our table.

Christ did as much the last time he ate with his friends on
the eve of his death. With simple gesture and spare words, he
broke the bread held in his hands and shared it with his
friends. His words they scarcely credited: 'This is my body.

103

Eat.' The same with the cup as he passed it over to them: 'My blood which I will shed for you. Drink. Remember me when you do this.'

This simple meal, which they hold at the sacred still centre of their life, has sustained Christians for two thousand years. Men have died for it. Gone in hiding to save its mystery. Travelled miles to secure its bounty. Named it in many guises: my favourite is the Old English, 'housel'.

Christ's own journey in life was purposeful and accomplished: nothing that had to be done was left undone. At the end, there was no last-minute rush. He had seen that everything was disposed according to his Father's will. His final gift? What else but himself: to be man's eternal and perfect prayer to the Father.

Man has no prayer save that of Jesus. The Son's prayer to his Father is his own death on the cross which we access and by which we are enfolded: the Eucharist.

*

Unlike the three Synoptics, John's Gospel contains no reference to the institution of the Eucharist; moreover, the evangelist sets the meal the day before the Passover. Neatly, he has altered the entire emphasis: it is Christ himself who is the new and fulfilling Pascal lamb: 'I am going now to prepare a place for you.' Matthew and Luke follow Mark's story of the disciples asking Jesus how they should prepare for the feast: He told them to go into the town, where they would see a man carrying a pitcher. (The mysterious and unexplained detail lends credibility to the story.) 'Tell him, the Lord has need of your room upstairs. That is where we will eat the Passover together.'

John, by contrast, has developed his understanding of Christ's death on the cross and, looking beyond the crude, outsider's image of a criminal death, he portrays the crucifixion as none other than a triumphant manifestation of God's master plan of love: 'If I am only lifted up, I will draw all men to me.' The room where the Last Supper took place becomes a detail to be set aside: it is Christ's own person, his own Body dying on the cross, raised up for all to see, that is now the place of sacrifice. Moreover, this is a once-and-for-all act of love and obedience accomplished by the Son at the word of his Father (just as Isaac submitted to Abraham's lifted sword and Abraham himself obeyed God's word).

The unique act of history.

Yet it is also a moment perduring for all time: by means of the sacramental signs of the bread and the wine, all men will come to share the one moment when Christ was obediently raised up. As Jesus prays in 'the priestly prayer' that opens John 17:

> Father, the hour has come:
> glorify your Son
> so that your Son may glorify you;
> and, through the power over all mankind that you have
> given him,
> let him give eternal life to all those you have entrusted to
> him.
> And eternal life is this:
> to know you,
> the only true God,
> and Jesus Christ whom you have sent.
> I have glorified you on earth
> and finished the work
> that you gave me to do.
> Now, Father, it is time for you to glorify me
> with that glory I had with you
> before ever the world was.

*

The Eucharist is the epicentre of each Parkminster day: at eight o'clock in the morning all attend the community Mass. The Prior or one of the three other priests presides as the whole community jointly celebrates the renewal of the passion of Christ and his saving work throughout the whole world. (Every priest will say their own Mass privately and alone later in the day.)

I was aching to join their Liturgy, drawn as to some special new experience of the Mass. I had heard a little about the Carthusian Mass. In London, long ago, the saying went: the London Charterhouse is where the Mass is really prayed. I remember at Wimbledon, before I joined the Society, coming across several mysterious mentions of St Ignatius and The Exercises in books about the Jesuits. 'What *are* The Exercises?' I asked my friend Father Hamer. In answer he pulled a slim book from his shelves. 'Here they are,' he said, 'but it is better not to read them: they will be *given* you in the noviceship.' Dom Cyril had intrigued me by referring to the Night Office as 'powerful prayer' and then to the morning Eucharist as being said 'mostly in silence'.

The first Mass I attended was in the evening of my second day, the eve of Saints Peter and Paul. It was sung and several priests concelebrated at the same time. There was a wonderful Asperges, the penitential cleansing of the congregation, when the priest sprinkles them, using the words of psalm 51: 'Purify me with hyssop until I am clean; wash me until I am whiter than snow.' Water was first blessed in a silver bucket by Dom Bruno with a singular prayer and large handfuls of rock salt that lay to hand in a John-the-Baptist scallop shell. God was thanked in resonant voice for giving us both elements, which were then mixed and stirred together.

The community then advanced almost at a trot to bow and be sploshed with the sacred stir. With a one, two, bow and away, we resembled those dispatch riders in circus rings who criss-cross in death-defying figures of eight. If we had missed our timing, there would have been a sure clash of heads.

The same process took place – quick march, left-right-left – the following Sunday. When I suddenly came face to face with Brother Christopher. Naturally, I signalled him through ahead of me. His face brightened. But then Ignace intervened: Christopher was to stay put. Doubtless, if he had advanced, the whole movement would have been thrown out of kilter. Heads would have cracked against each other in all the wrong places!

*

My first morning Eucharist the very next day was in different mode. Mass is always sung, using the ancient Latin plainsong version of the proper, yet the daily celebration remains starkly simple. The altar is a plain table at the head of the choir stalls, yet the focal point of the first part of the Mass – the liturgy of the word – is centred on the reading lectern, with the monks facing each other outwards in their stalls. As with everything Carthusian, both gesture and ritual are simple. But nothing can conceal that coming together in order to celebrate the Eucharist presents the sum total of their life aim. If the Carthusian seeks to be closer each day to the Father, modelling himself on Christ's life, this bread and wine is the very sustenance of his journey. More, the enactment of Christ's free gift of himself on Calvary is for the monk a source of wonder, of thanks and his consummate goal. There is no hiding the truth that, as the Carthusian is in love with God, this is where he finds him. Mass is unmistakably intimate and private, although enacted by the whole community. Its central passage, the canon of the Mass from the sanctus to the Pater Noster, is prayed in silence, the community at their stalls in upright prayer. At the moment of the consecration, all kneel. The Host is raised. High above the priest's head, a great brown numinous disc, wafted in real time while an age is held.

Now, as the priest reaches for the great silver goblet to take hold of its two side-handles, each monk prostrates to lie upon his side in the Carthusian manner – an almost foetal tuck – while the chalice is elevated unseen. His prayer to Christ might be the *Anima Christi,* those mediaeval words, 'In your own wounds hide me; never let me part from you . . .'

An engraving in the guesthouse shows 'The Mass of the Holy Spirit' celebrated by Prior Houghton with his community of the London Charterhouse on the day when he and two companions were carted off to meet their bloody execution at Tyburn. We are told that as the Host was raised, all present felt a rush and noise of the Holy Spirit among them, Christ's promised Advocate.

I do not much admire the picture, which is a literal and wan statement of what took place that day. Yet the artist cannot help himself in understating that moment which no images, no words can possibly portray. It is Christ's invitation to the curious young man who had met him by the lakeside: 'Master,' he begged, 'where are you based?' 'Come and see' was Jesus' reply.

Seeing and praying the Mass with these men makes words seem inadequate.

*

I was puzzled at the singing. Or the lack of it. Gone was the bullish to and fro of the Night Office. Now all was diffidence and hanging back. The deputed cantor was left to carry the day.

Familiar with the first plainsong text, a votive Mass of the Holy Name that was identical to the proper for the Mass of St Ignatius, I joined in confidently on that second morning. The next day was a Mass of the dead with which, once more, I was familiar. And then it occurred to me that their style was not to 'perform' so much as to pray the Mass; it was not necessary to attempt a massed choir of the Rhondda Valley effect. Here it was different. We were in 'real time', the time of birth and of death, when man finds his clock has ceased and he is without time as normally experienced in this new, stretched moment. As more than one mediaeval hymn puts it, 'Thine age at Mass shall not increase.'

When we listen again to Christ's own words of promise, none of this can come as a surprise:

If you only knew what God is offering
and who it is that is saying to you:
Give me a drink,
you would have been the one to ask,
and he would have given you living water . . .
I tell you most solemnly,
it was not Moses who gave you bread from heaven,
it is my Father who gives you the bread from heaven,
the true bread;
for the bread of God

is that which comes down from heaven
and gives life to the world . . .
I tell you most solemnly,
if you do not eat the flesh of the Son of Man
and drink his blood,
you will not have life in you.
Anyone who does eat my flesh and drink my blood
has eternal life,
and I shall raise him up on the last day.
John 4:10; 6:32-33, 53-54

*

The Carthusians' liturgical calendar is relatively uncluttered. Never prone to proclaim their own saints, they enjoy a wide freedom to choose a variety of 'votive' Masses, each with a different petition and liturgical theme. (St Hugh was their first formal saint, canonized not by his own Order but at the insistence of the Church at large when he died, as the much-loved Bishop of Lincoln. Even Bruno himself only became a saint by the back door: two centuries after his death, the Carthusians asked the Pope if they might solemnize his feast-day of 6th October. His response was to canonize their founder without further process.)

In a typical week, Masses might be said of the Holy Spirit and of St Joseph, then a Mass for the dead, or a Mass for vocations – a quiet gesture of welcome for a new postulant. Each Mass bears its own special message, setting the central Eucharistic prayer in a fresh framework each day. These specially chosen Masses will be regularly interspersed with the major feast-days as they occur within the calendar – Saints Peter and Paul, St Benedict, the feast of St Bruno. All these feasts likewise carry their own burden of news, which has been heralded in the preceding Night Office to link it with the dawn Mass ahead.

*

The modern rite of the Carthusian Mass contains several hall-marks retained from mediaeval days. One is their endearing *confiteor* or confession of sins, where each monk beats his breast thrice with the words: 'For I have sinned gravely through my fault, through my pride, through my thoughts, through my words, through my deeds . . .' Their one certain sin, they declare, is pride.

The kiss of peace is passed down from the priest in a rippling chain of contact that is still very formal and unsmiling. But if Vincent – the Ibo from Nigeria, with his great beaming smile – has his way, it will not be long before it is exchanged with a good deal more visible human warmth.

After Communion, which is taken as the entire community gathers around the priest and encircles the altar, there comes ten minutes of silent, private prayer of thanksgiving, with everyone, including the celebrant, seated in their stalls. The Mass ends with a blessing, each monk signing himself in the Carthusian manner, thumb held stiff, the first and second fingers put together apart from the folded hand. Then all kneel while Communion is taken to the sick still confined to their cells – Brother Richard attending the priest with warning bell and ancient brass lantern.

As soon as Mass is over, everyone except the sacristan leaves the church. The Statutes make special mention that no one should stay behind in the church to pray. There is work to do. Now the day has started.

IX

WALKING ABROAD

> That very same day, two of them were on their way to a
> village called Emmaus . . . and they were talking together
> about all that had happened. Now as they talked this over,
> Jesus himself came up and walked by their side.
> *Luke 24:13*

My last day at Parkminster was to be my best day, not because
I was leaving for home, but because I was to join the community in their monthly walk. Every Monday the choir monks
lunch early and then, still clad in their white habits, set off into
the Sussex countryside for a long walk, beginning at noon
and returning in time for late Vespers at about five. But once a
month, they are joined by the brothers and postulant novices
when the whole community sallies forth. I had been keen to
join their company, since it would provide me with a legitimate opportunity of meeting the monks and talking freely
with them at their most relaxed. I had already suggested such
a possibility to Father Prior on our first meeting, but I got
nowhere. He seemed to look through me with neither yes nor
no.

But now the Prior was away in hospital and not expected
back for a few days. In his absence, Dom Bruno, the Vicar, was
in charge. I had not spoken to him throughout my stay,
although I felt I knew him well. He it was who had gathered
me in when, on the first night of my stay, I had stood hesi-
tating outside the church, waiting for the community to file in
ahead of me. I had been startled, then delighted, when
without hesitation, he came up to me saying, 'Now don't
stand around there in the cold – come along inside.' (I had
been reared on a somewhat more absolute Jesuit interpreta-

tion of *magnum silentium*, the night silence that must never be violated.) He led me down the full length of the church and saw me into my choir stall with much courtesy, only then taking his own place beside the Prior's stall as the cantor on our side.

On Saturday afternoon at around 3.15, I went to his cell to seek my necessary permission to join the walk. I pulled the bell, which tinkled faintly from some secret inner recess. He greeted me warmly and ushered me through his ambulacrum and out into the garden. He was genuinely pleased to meet me: 'I did not wish to interfere between the Prior and yourself,' he boomed. I sensed at once that he somehow felt responsible for the future contents of my book. His position as archivist of Parkminster's history follows logically from his now being the longest serving member of the community. He joined in 1946, after wartime service in the Royal Navy. His manner is jovial and expansive, and he uses his voice with full-lunged enjoyment. We stood talking in the warm July sun in his flagrantly neglected garden, mercilessly overtaken by weeds and thistles. As my eye took in the wilderness, he explained his all-too-obvious neglect. Although seeming hale and hearty, he had had a severe crisis some two years ago. He began to put on weight alarmingly and eventually his heart became suspect. At length, his doctor pinned it down to an allergy to the home-brewed cider. But accompanying this physical trouble came a deep depression and loss of confidence. 'I could not celebrate a public Mass. I could do nothing.' But he slowly picked up and today is back in full form, so that the outsider would never have guessed the seriousness of his recent setback. I forgave him the generous crop of weeds in his sunbathed garden.

We moved on to other topics, notably my book. He offered to fill me in with the history of Parkminster. And I asked if we could talk at some length on my next visit. Finally, I asked about joining the community walk on my last day.

'You must go – for the sake of the book. It is essential for your research.' I smiled at his exuberance and thanked him warmly, feeling as if several notable indulgences had been included in this fulsome permission. But then, to my dismay, suddenly he qualified: 'But if the Prior returns before Monday, he will then be superior, so that you must go and ask his permission.' He added that he had telephoned the hospital that morning to learn that Father Cyril had a temperature and could well be kept in over the weekend. I warmed to the idea, not fancying my chances so well with the Prior.

I found Father Bruno at his weekly task of compiling a sheet of prayer intentions to be pinned up each Sunday on the noticeboard outside church. And before I left, I asked him about the concern expressed the previous week about Rupert Murdoch's price war on Fleet Street. We had been urged to pray that his ambitions 'to take over the thought processes of the nation' be thwarted. I suggested that Murdoch's only ambition was to make money, and having done so, to make yet more money. I challenged the idea that he had the least wish to take over every little paper in the land or even turn them out of business. I tried to go into detail about rival circulations and windows in the market share, but felt I was making little headway, and we agreed to differ.

It was a good example of the complexities of my life, where the more that is said, the less is understood. The Carthusian viewpoint was simple: the rich, multinational entrepreneur was to be resisted at every turn of his ambitions.

On Sunday evening, a washed-out Prior limped into church for Vespers; a slow smile seemed to play around his lips. I was pleased to see him safely back from hospital, but I now had a dilemma of obedience. Back in the kitchen, I consulted Benedict: should I just duck and go on the walk, or must I ask the Prior? He was adamant that I needed the Prior's word, adding 'And I think he may say no. In fact, I think I would say no. Outsiders just don't go on walks.' I mused about all this and decided that I would not make the Prior's life any more difficult. He had enough problems coming back as superior; in any case, he was still recuperating and hardly wanted me hammering on his door. Perhaps I just could not face the rejection of a 'No'. I decided I would simply go home quietly on Monday morning. But at the end of Mass on that last morning, the Prior came past my stall and slipped one of his diminutive notes on my pew. It read simply: '† July 12. Dear John, The Walk OK. Bon voyage. Peace and Joy. † Cyril.' I was on the walk.

We ate an early lunch at 10.30. No food or drink is taken on the regular weekly walks; although once a year, there is an extra-long walk when a grand picnic is organized halfway through the day up on the Downs. It was already a hot July day and at lunch, camel-wise, I made sure to take on board a good deal of water.

At 11.30 we gathered in the Brothers' chapel for walk prayers. I had had no previous occasion to enter this place and was intrigued to discover it full-blown baroque, its interior an overall cold blue. It made a striking contrast with the austerity of the church and seemed to be making a statement about the divergent perceptions of the two communities, the choir monks and the *conversi*. Dominating the altar was a central niche containing a life-size statue of Our Lady. I winced involuntarily when presently a brother entered the chapel and flicked a switch to illuminate her as the centre of attraction. Most of the community had already arrived. I knelt beside Joseph and shared a prayer sheet. After a few familiar responses, we sat down and Dom Bernard began a short reading. The chapel was full of echoes, and I did not follow his meaning, except to recognize a joke about monks in the tail end. A ripple of amusement flowed around the chapel, but I was unable to hear the punchline: I would try to remember to ask him chapter and verse later.

We trooped out of chapel to gather outside the front door of the monastery. I looked around at my companions in some disbelief: we were a wonderfully ragamuffin group. It was clear from footwear alone that The Walk was serious business. Well-shined boots, verging on Doc. Martin's, were in evidence among the younger members; stout sticks and sunhats signalled senior members' intentions not to be outdone. Dom Aloysius, rendered almost half-size under a generously brimmed sunhat, clutched a walking stick in either hand, his chin stuck out resolutely, a challenge to anyone who would disqualify his candidature in this event. The monks wore their habits. Then I looked again: these were disguise habits, distinctly theatrical in their origins; skimpy and light-weight tokens, they appeared to be made up of discarded sheets. The postulants were dressed in assorted lay clothes of their own choice which only added to the general air of motley.

Ignace now took command; his dominating height and indisputable bulk registered that he was the 'superior' of the walk. Ignace had been next to me in choir, and I had heard a little about his background from the Prior. A Belgian, he had been set for an international career as a concert organist when he had conceived the single purpose of becoming a Carthusian. He was yet one more example of the fully international mixture of the Parkminster community. A discernible, bubbling levity took over the company, as he read out who would walk with who, two by two, for a period of twenty minutes at a time. Ignace, with all the wisdom of his new role as superior, had designated me as his first companion. And I fell into step with this amiable giant, whom I had previously known only as an adjacent voice in choir.

Barely two years out of Belgium he may be, but his command of English is excellent, any deficiencies being amply covered by a wicked sense of verbal fun. For the remainder of the day, it was up to me to set together the patchwork of stories and impressions, whatever I might glean from this unique succession of peripatetic interviews. I asked Ignace the reason for his choice of a Jesuit name in religion. He replied that it had been in honour of an uncle who had influenced him greatly. We had not been long together before I realized that he imagined I had come to join the Order. I put him right by tapping my wedding ring and confessed that I had merely come to write a book. He responded enthusiastically by telling me the story of his decision to join the Carthusians and the accompanying media interest.

Not only had he forsaken a promising music career as solo organist just as he was beginning to become internationally recognized, but he had also left his fiancée behind. In Belgium there was considerable media interest, with both newspapers and television looking for an exclusive on his story. Knowing the Carthusian tradition of silence, he declined to satisfy any of these approaches. But one day, he felt so pestered that he telephoned the Belgian cardinal to ask his advice. Cardinal Daniel responded firmly. This was a story that would do the Church good and was worth telling; whatever the known reluctance on the part of the Carthusians, he should go ahead and talk to the media, giving them in detail the reasons for his decision to break with both his fiancée and his career. One television company in particular had attracted him; the presenter seemed considerate and keen to achieve a balanced story. A deal was brokered: there would be film clips of Ignace playing the organ plus interviews, firstly with himself and his fiancée, then with his parents. The programme, he declared, would come out in the autumn, and he would never see it, merely hear reviews and second-hand reports.

All this Ignace told me in the context of my own book. Publicity for the Carthusians was good for them, he thought, and they certainly had a story to tell. He mentioned a book written about La Grande Chartreuse by two journalists from *Paris Match*. At first, he had thought it pretentious: they had taken the line that this was the scoop of the century: never before had any human penetrated the secrets of the Carthusians. But on balance, he declared it to be a fair and representative account of their life and mores.

We had been walking a rutted bridleway and now came to a five-barred gate. Ignace paused; all the weight of his superior's office bore down upon him as he consulted his walking map with great care. But presently, Dom Aloysius came alongside and confidently indicated that the path continued through the wood.

It was time to change partners. Each monk thanked the other by name for his company before learning the identity of his next walking brother. I was immensely struck by the simple, singular attention each afforded the other. I had imagined that on being let loose into the countryside, the hermit might look about him to admire its beauties. I discovered that all their energies were directed to the other person, their companion of

116

the moment. It was not a false or even polite attitude, but one that seemed fulfilled with real love and affection.

As we gathered round a second time, I reflected that twenty minutes had gone so swiftly. Ignace made a great fuss and joke of singing out the new pairings. Each time, he enjoyed the performance: he had some system of index cards which he shuffled clumsily in his fist like a third-rate conjurer. In an act of self-parody that still enjoyed the performance for its own sake, he would address himself sometimes as Saint Ignace or then switch this handle to some other person with considerable comic effect; or now he would pretend to get it all wrong, stumble to a halt and then have to start again. He was bubbling the whole time with the pleasure of renewing his facility of playing to an audience, and finding it hugely amusing. Harmlessly infectious, we all enjoyed his idiocies. As soon as the new companies were settled, he would study his map briefly and then plunge ahead like a general leading some military exercise, declaring that we must keep up the pace so as to hold to our schedule.

Now I was walking with Vincent, the wonderfully recollected Ibo boy who is so radiant at Mass each morning as he receives and passes on the kiss of peace. (I had noticed this phenomenon early during my stay and began to look out for it and enjoy it each morning. While the rest of the community enacted the pax stiffly with much reverence and a solemn face, Vincent could not help but open his great white-toothed smile and radiate undiluted human love as he embraced his brothers on either side.)

Curious to know how he had found his way to Parkminster, I asked him how he had learned about the Carthusians in Nigeria. There are some monastic communities back home, he assured me; he himself had been with the Trappists for a time. At once he described how their quarters afforded little privacy, the walls were so thin that every noise could be heard through them. 'The only time you could really be alone to pray was during siesta,' he complained. He was soon set on pursuing the contemplative life to the full. He came upon the Carthusians in a book; they seemed to be everything he asked for. It was only a small step to England! He is in his early twenties and is immersed in an alien culture far from home – a culture, moreover, that reaches back into Europe's mediaeval past, ignorant of the riches of Africa. Yet I can detect no inkling of discomfort at the strange lifestyle that has engulfed him since he came to Parkminster. He works with quiet energy at all the tasks he is set, leaving Benedict to comment that he has never known anyone like him.

With limited English, Vincent maintains a very direct manner of communication. He thought I should seek an *imprimatur* for my book, indicating that the Bishop's office judged it free from doctrinal error. I shuddered and patiently explained that I wanted to reach the widest possible audience and that his suggestion of episcopal approval, helpfully though it was intended, might put too many people off. He conceded my point readily. Vincent's English is still hesitant, his pronunciation uncertain. And I found it hard to follow all he was trying to tell me. Communication is a serious problem that runs deep within this silent international community. The majority of newcomers arrive with halting English pronunciation. English lessons are offered, but in a community where normal conversation is rare and English is read rather than spoken, it is an uphill task to improve. Moreover, public readings are continually performed in a broad range of foreign mispronunciations – all brave attempts, to be sure, yet most fall long or short of the target of received English. Listening to the readings in church, I experienced constant difficulty interpreting the meaning of some brethren as they struggled to offer good account of words still unfamiliar to them. If this felt to my English ear like some kind of aural jigsaw puzzle, piecing together the sense as each word fell, how fared the rest of the audience, I wondered. (Some of these misgivings have already been answered by an investment in new books by the Prior in order to support a fresh initiative in English teaching.)

We came to a well-cared-for cricket field; the club groundsman stood up from whitelining the boundary and greeted us as we straggled by. I asked Vincent if he was familiar with our

118

national game. But it seemed he had barely heard of it. His eyes were more full of wonder for the close-mown grass; nothing he had ever walked upon before had been greener and smoother. His eyes widened in disbelief as he tip-toed reverentially across this strange English field.

The woods were left behind, and we began to pass along the banks of a canal, where canny herons lifted up on lazy wing. It was the first time I had properly taken in my surroundings. I looked around to see that, unlike me, every monk was absorbed, not in the scenic splendours all around – the great rolling Downs presiding over all this rare helping of the great outside world – but intent upon enjoying the human companionship of his walking fellow. Each had left his hermitage for the day, but it was not to gawp at hills and rivers and wild landscapes. The chief and sole recreation was the pleasure of communing with another man's soul.

I was next to pair with Joseph, the young Filipino boy, my early companion in the kitchen, a novice postulant still waiting to take the habit. Compact and handsome at five foot six, today he had dressed in white jeans and a teeshirt. There was something immensely neat about this turn-out that put me in mind of a US sailor on shore-leave. He too carried a walking-stick, out of place for a young man, yet token that he shared to the full the expedition's purpose. He laughed readily and I enjoyed feeding him jokes. We had dropped to the tail end of the file, and he told me in mock earnest that this is always the place of the first importance. The Prior always brings up the rear, he assured me. I at once declared that I was Prior and he could be Procurator. We gave blessings to imaginary well-wishers as we passed along.

I asked him about his family and how he came to Parkminster. His family were uppermost in his mind: a letter had arrived that morning. His mother had been unwell and had undergone lengthy hospital treatment but was now recovered. He spoke about the cost of health in his country; then about his siblings – none of whom were active Christians. Joseph was the eldest in the family; a younger brother was studying law and his sister was married. Once again, the

119

familiar story: he learned about the Carthusians by chance and was immediately attracted. He began as a postulant with the Charterhouse in Vermont, USA, which had been founded from Europe in the 1950s. He was not easily drawn on this experience, apart from saying that he was far happier at Parkminster. The Americans were very directive, he hinted, whereas in England he felt accepted as one of the community. But why did he transfer to England? He was told simply that his visa had expired.

Then suddenly the conversation deepened. We spoke of his vocation, of his desire to persevere. He told me of the system that would admit him to the community as a novice: at the end of his six months' postulancy, the professed of the community would vote in chapter. A majority of two thirds would enable him to join them and take the Carthusian habit as a brother. If the vote were to be against him, then he would have to leave. I told him that I would vote twice for him and that I was certain he will have no difficulty.

In the event, he was accepted, with no hesitation. But that is not always the case. One recent example seems to have rocked the community. A professional man with his career behind him sought to join the community. He had been married and was the father of three adult children; but the marriage had broken down some years before and now he wanted to try his vocation at Parkminster. He first applied through La Grande Chartreuse for the necessary dispensation from Rome, which after due deliberation was given; and at length he arrived at Parkminster. He was a competent musician and became convinced that he could help reform the singing in choir. The only problem was that he failed to convince sufficient numbers of the community. It was said that both the Prior and Vicar voted in his favour, but there was nothing they could do when the vote went against him. Here, I realized, was the ultimate check and balance of a group of men bound to live harmoniously together: the community as a whole accepts each new member, or as in this case, they may decline acceptance. No wonder Joseph felt apprehensive about his imminent election.

We moved on to his experience of the inner life. He knew that he must suffer and sometimes find himself down in spirit, and that was hard. I likened it to marriage and told him this too was hard work and needed continual effort and perseverance. You don't escape life's rub by coming to a monastery, we both agreed. 'What sort of spirituality do you have, John?' he asked of a sudden. Joseph is deliciously direct. I replied that I was in favour of the Trinity and prayed to Our Lady a good deal. I felt a bit of a fraud but genuinely wished to build his courage. I will grieve mightily should Joseph leave Parkminster.

Twenty minutes had already gone and I now walked with Hugh. Hugh the gentle, Hugh the hesistant. Hugh, whose bright, innocent eyes were forever full of good will and humour. He was a brother who helped in the pantry and looked after visitors. He told me of the annual long walk that would take place the following Monday. It is an all-day affair when a mini-bus is hired to take the community further afield. He points to the South Downs rising ahead: 'You see that clump of trees? That's Chanctonbury Ring, or what's left of it after the great storm of '87.' That route was Hugh's favourite walk. But the next week they would walk an alternative circuit upon the North Downs, which he liked less. He described the routine: the bus delivers the combatants to their starting-point, from which they walk out to a rendezvous around midday. Less able-bodied brethren remain in the bus, which takes them on to the picnic spot. And at lunch-time, they all assemble for a great picnic – Hugh became animated in his description – of cream cakes and beer and cider and lemonade. The somewhat prep. school menu was listed with relish and in full. Then various anecdotes tumbled out: how two years ago, the weather had turned nasty and a vote was taken whether to abandon the walk or to continue. Only one voice dissented from continuing, and then the storm broke. Hugh was wearing a plastic sack with a hole for his head and secured about his waist with string – a poor man's cagoule. As they bowed into the lashing rain, it turned to hail. Before his astonished gaze his protective plastic was slowly ripped and shredded, and checking with the rest, he saw they fared no better. They finally reached the coach soaked to the skin.

Then there was the time Dom Aloysius had become so tired along the route that it was agreed he should sit by the roadside to await the minibus as it made its way past to the lunch-time picnic spot. So Aloysius pulled his cowl over his head and, knowing him, fell into deep prayer with his Maker. Presently a Morris Traveller passed by. It stopped, and out jumped a young woman, who went to investigate this strange roadside apparition. Who knows what she expected to find within this white bundle of rags? Lifting the cowl, she took one look at what lay beneath and uttered a loud shriek. She ran screaming back to her car and drove off fast!

Hugh told me that he had been eleven years a donate and had only taken the habit three years before, when Dom Cyril had arrived to take office as Prior. A donate is a full member of the community who lives the Carthusian rule in so far as he is able; yet, since for technical reasons, such as health, he is not able, for example, to attend the Night Office regularly, he is not permitted to take the habit. But in Hugh's case there were no reasons why he should not be admitted to profession; merely he had never been invited. It is quite as easy, it seems, to get overlooked and become a fixture and fitting in a monastery as anywhere else. Hugh told me this quite factually, without any semblance of surprise or complaint at the way his life as a monk had worked out. Indeed, any element of criticism in my account of his case is registered solely by me.

I was reminded of the death notice that had been pinned up on the noticeboard outside the church two days previously. Carthusians worldwide signal each other to pray for their deceased brethren. This news came from the former Yugoslavia and, according to custom, was posted in Latin:

Karel Zemlzic,
Vedanae . . .
aetatis suae anno 77
donationis suae 53
professionis vero 21.

Joining the Carthusian house of Pleterje at the age of twenty-four, he had been a donate for over thirty years before finally being admitted to profession at the age of fifty-six. Here was another journey of discovery that lies untold: Vedano, the young Karel's birthplace, is twenty miles outside Grozny in Chechnya and all of one thousand miles from the monastery in Yugoslavia where he lived all his adult life and died.

Dom Bernard was my next companion. One of the most senior members of the community, Bernard is a craggy Irishman who could have just strode down from his hill farm in Kerry, sheepdog to heel, walking staff in hand to put the kettle on his hob and take tea with a neighbour. During the war he was a GP, working both in England and Wales, but as soon as peace came, he joined the Irish Cistercians at Nunraw. Inevitably, he was soon appointed infirmarian with the cure of some 200 monks. He remained a Cistercian for fourteen years, but at length his hankering after a more contemplative life brought him to the Carthusians. He had been Prior at Parkminster for seven years but was now, to his relief, a simple choir monk once more. He spoke feelingly of the burdens of being an 'officer' and confessed that he was by nature no organizer. He did not know the purpose of my visit, so I explained; I hoped to achieve a solid book about the community that attempted to reveal their still centre and purpose. Answering his question, I told him I was married with four grown-up children. This led him to speak feelingly of marriages where love was lost between the partners and the damage this caused to their children. Dom Bernard insisted that a necessary part of the contemplative's make-up was a deep experience of self-worth derived from having been loved unconditionally by one's parents. In this way, he is led to faith in God's overwhelming and unconditional love for him.

We moved on to name Jesuits that we might both know, ending up with Father Jimmy Walsh, who had made a life-long study of the English mystics. Here was someone I knew well. He had taught me when I was a boy at Wimbledon, where I had sung in his choir. Later I had joined the Society with his younger brother, Frank. There was only one difficulty

– I looked across, catching my companion's gaunt profile, his prominent nose, capped by thick horn-rimmed spectacles: 'But he's dead,' was all I could say. There came a moment of unreality; if Dom Bernard, who knew him well, did not know of his death, how could I be certain? For just those few seconds, I was completely unsure of my facts. And then I rationalized that between the two of us, perhaps I might be expected to be the better informed.

In another reshuffle, I now walked with Dom Aloysius, the Swiss German priest who intrigued and fascinated me. We introduced ourselves and he was taken by my name. 'Skinner? Skinner . . .' trying the sound, wrinkling his nose and making my name float up in the hot summer air. 'What is that?'

I countered that it was a trade name, and made as if to peel potatoes. As soon as he understood, he returned at once to his own name with something akin to triumph. 'And I am Little Rose!' He seemed delighted that whereas my name was curious, his own was little short of ridiculous. 'Rösli!' he added with emphasis.

At this I was bidden round to his right shoulder – 'My good ear is there' – and off we sallied. We came to a stile, and I had to bundle his recalcitrant, stick-like legs over for him. We were on our way again, falling behind the company all the while.

'Do you know how long I have been a monk?' came his question quite unexpectedly. It was something of a test, for if I said too short a time, he would be disappointed; if I overshot, he would then be obliged to issue a correction which would lead to the same result. (I had noticed that everyone in the monastery keeps their exact tally of days.)

'I can't guess,' I weaved, and, to my relief, it worked.

'Forty-one years,' he replied.

Encouraged, I plunged on: 'And in all that time, what has been the hardest thing?' I felt like a *Daily Mail* journalist: as soon as I opened my mouth, I wished I had not spoken. There came a pause that only increased my anxiety. This was the last person I wished to offend.

Each morning at the end of my first week, Dom Aloysius had celebrated the conventual Mass. His attitude is totally prayerful; he seems taken up into the solemn enactment of Christ's passion. At the elevation of the Host, it is as if he sees Christ in Person on the cross. His face shows utter devotion and reverence and appears almost waxen and transparent. At Communion he brings the Bread to each member of the community in turn as they stand in a half circle before the altar. He looks you in the eye and with immense love utters the words, 'The Body of Christ.'

At last the reply came: 'Putting up with all my many sins.'

I looked straight ahead, even more aware of the figure walking beside me: little Aloysius, frail, undaunted, a stick in both hands, his ascetic head stuck into a faded buff sunhat. The concept of sin seemed far away; yet I believed him. There must be many shades of sin.

We had come to a wheat field barring our way. Our leader, nothing daunted, began to shepherd his flock around its perimeter. I was reminded of the scene in St Matthew when the disciples, walking with Jesus on the Sabbath, pick the husks and begin eating them, only to be challenged by the Pharisees. It is one of those harmless snapshot moments that suddenly come alive to us across the centuries.

He went on to tell me of the regular visits of Lord Cheshire. Aloysius wasn't one to *tutoyer* Leonard Cheshire. 'I shook his hand,' he said proudly. I was fairly certain that Cheshire too would have noted the encounter. He went on to tell me of his generosity when a member of the community had suffered a brain tumour and the wish was to nurse him at home. He arranged for professional advice on designing the sick monk's cell. And Cell A, on the ground floor nearest to the brothers' quarters, was converted. It remains the sick man's cell, and at present Brother Gabriel is quartered there, waiting to die. Finally, I was able to thank Aloysius for the courteous way he had given me Communion on several occasions. 'Not at all: it is a great privilege for me too,' he clipped out in his Swiss English. It was all change once more.

Robert comes from Slovakia, a country I always associate

with storytelling. I told him I had been a children's bookseller. His eyes gleamed and he became animated. 'Then do you have Astrid Lindgren – Pippi Longstocking?' I said of course she was translated into English, adding that I would send him a couple of books to improve his English. Whereupon he whooped and clapped me on the back in sheer delight. I can hardly remember a child customer of mine ever having been so enthusiastic!

I asked him how on earth he had found Parkminster from the depths of Europe. By the age of twenty-four, he had finished his computer programming studies and had started his first job. 'I completed my first project, artificial intelligence. And then I knew I wanted to be a contemplative.' He joked about computers driving him to solitude. But it was true solitude he wanted. There are monasteries in Slovakia, and by chance he met a Cistercian with whom he discussed his ambitions. But he was put off by this monk being away from his monastery. Then finally he wrote to the Prior at La Grande Chartreuse. The reply came back promptly – a negative, since he had no French; but he was invited to write to the English Charterhouse. He had been at Parkminster now for almost ten months; it would soon be time for his parents to come and visit him. They were both quite elderly, he told me; he was anxious about the rigours of their journey, which they would be making by non-stop coach.

By this time we had come to a crossroads; the path either went straight ahead or took a left turn through a farmyard. Ahead of us, Ignace halted with his companion, Bogdan, to consult the map. The four of us were by now well ahead of the field, the others nowhere in sight. After consultation with a farmhand, it was decided that we must cut through the yard towards Lock Farm. Off we set, our doubts resolved.

Now it was the hottest time of the day. We paced out, engrossed in our twin conversations, until we arrived at a pleasant house with a sizeable artificial pond in its front garden. Two stout Labradors on short legs came over to sniff us and say hello. We gathered by the roadside in the shade of an oak to await the rest of the party. They came in slowly, now two, now two more. When suddenly a single white-garbed figure came striding out towards us.

It was Dom Bernard, his face set far from fair.

He made a beeline for Ignace and without drawing breath, began to tear him apart. He was the superior of the walk, and he had acted disgracefully. He had not waited for the party before taking the last left turn, and this had led to chaos. No one had known which way to go.

His anger was emphasized by its full-throated Irish utterance.

It was all very embarrassing. I felt for Ignace, and yet it was entirely justified. Bernard had left Aloysius behind to catch us up, and we waited some while in uncomfortable and desultory conversation until at length he arrived. I guessed that perhaps a little pantomime would lighten the mood. So I bade Ignace kneel in the middle of the track. As Aloysius came up, I borrowed his stick and declared that Ignace should receive a penance across his shoulders. But Aloysius would have none of this, and bent down to kiss his right shoulder. It was all a bit daft, but at least it sent the storm clouds scudding.

Ignace read out yet another set of companions: this time, his manner was subdued. I walked with Jim, who at once offered a brief account of his background that was again as varied as any. A former student from Osterley, the London crammer college run by the Jesuits for men who come late to the priesthood, he knew several people who had joined the Jesuit novitiate with me in the fifties. He too had thought about the Society; but he explained that at the time his mother had been ill, and he thought it kinder to stay close at hand. Joining the Edinburgh diocese, he was ordained priest in the early sixties. He had later left the priesthood and married, to find his career in the prison service and ending up as a governor. He and his wife had four children. They were almost all grown up, as he was nearing retirement; but he had been so successful that he was pressed to stay on in the service for a further term. Two years ago, without warning, Margaret, his wife, went down with cancer of the breast and chest and died within a few months. Two years on, Jim still grieves for his wife every day, declaring that he took her for granted. He is a donate, and while he leads the full life of the community, he is unlikely ever to take the habit as a professed monk. His talents were recognized when he was recently appointed Procurator of the house, an onerous and distracting office. Jim spoke hopefully of being allowed to say Mass once more. It is a permission of some gravity that can only come directly from Rome. He expressed the view that he would need to keep his head down until the next Pope was elected. John Paul II has always maintained a hard line with priests who resign their orders. For many years, he refused to treat with their cases in any way, content to leave them in some hard Limbo, hoping for their return to duty. It was a decision that left many good men who still wished to remain within the Church high and dry without the sacraments; while those who had been fortunate enough to leave the priesthood under his predecessor enjoyed full dispensation from their priestly vows, even enabling them to marry solemnly within the Church. Jim, leaving while Paul VI was Pope, had at least been among their number.

I was now accompanying Bogdan, the Polish priest and novice whose onions had just been harvested and whose lettuce I had picked the week before. I was at once curious to ask him about his cell, which I had found so attractive. First, the imitation foliage that so beautifully framed St Hugh. Bogdan was noncommittal: 'I found two or three branches.' (At once, he made it sound a simple task that anyone could undertake.) 'Then I tied poplar leaves with cotton . . .' I asked about the wonderful nutmeg colour, but was met with: 'You should have seen them at first. They were red and orange. Many wonderful colours.' Bogdan fell silent in the memory. 'I must do them again soon . . .' But this still left unanswered the miraculously stiff presentation of each leaf, standing bold against the white wall behind and perfectly showing off the little white porcelain image of Hugh and his friendly swan. The man was either a genius at a new genre of flower arrangement or angels helped him in his labours. It was not for me to pry further.

I moved on to another item to slake my curiosity, the wall-bar lashed above his stairwell. Yes, he admitted, it was 'to pull myself on'. (I pictured him like some ancient Roman martyr, his solid, well-knit torso, hanging there stretched out for long periods at a time.) And then the throw-away line: 'You see, with the hard bed, the back needs to be put straight again.' I absorbed this stoic Slav statement in silence. My impressions of Bogdan flashed out in my mind – the ascetic solitary, fashioning his private path of self-denial. I asked him about his work in Warsaw. Did he have his own parish? 'But I was only a vicar,' he offered modestly. Bogdan is thirty-two years of age: he could easily spend the next fifty years at Parkminster. And he gives every impression that he will do just that.

By now we were completing our wide arc and approaching the outskirts of Henfield, with the church spire looming near again from time to time. We came upon a series of lanes that wove their uncertain paths through a succession of large houses, each one well set in its own rambling garden. A fresh halt was called. The map was consulted across a five-barred gate at the entrance to a pleasing red-brick villa. By now the company had bunched together with the more modest walking pace. We began to reassemble, ragged yet content. Our several conversations began to peter out as separate possibilities and now came together like some swelling stream in a collective murmur of well-being.

Dogs emerged and tumbled up the driveway to challenge our presence with a cacophony of mounting barks. We stood our ground and soon they sounded inconsolable. Slowly and with deliberate steps that were at first hard to interpret, their lady owner gradually approached her front gate. My first thoughts came that she would chide us for disturbing the peace. But the broad smile across her face belied any such thoughts of crossness. She came on quietly surveying us, as if savouring the moment. Then she spoke with the slightest hint of a reproof:

'You used to come regularly and walk all around here. But that was twenty years ago. I haven't seen you since.'

She came up and stood by her gate, gazing at our white-robed crew with undisguised affection. She suggested letting her dogs through the gate. They would sniff us, she explained, but then stop their barking. She did so, and we continued our exchanges. A certain guilt had crept in on our side of the gate that inadvertently we had neglected her.

'Where have you been?' she insisted.

We looked around in dismay, our glances eventually falling upon Aloysius. Surely he would remember creeping unseen past this gate not too long ago. But he felt sure that he had never been that way his whole life past. Compounding his neglect, he explained how the community walked out each week, taking a choice of different routes.

I could be passing certain that this good lady owed no overt Christian allegiance. Yet what was unmistakable was her striking acceptance that this straggle of white-clad monks was totally benign; passing her gate this day, they would bring sure blessings on her household, both now and throughout the coming winter. Her chickens would lay, her children prosper, her husband rest content.

We lingered a few moments more, to take directions that she spelt out over the rambler's map spread wide upon her gate. The dogs had by now completed their ankle tour and for their pains received countless attentions from everyone in sight. We moved on. Yet as we took the footpath that circled her property and began to resume our paired conversations – with difficulty, since here we went single file and must call out over our shoulders – she came running towards us down the length of her back garden. For a moment of vainglory, I believed she was asking for a photo call. Instead, in spite of her careful directions, we were taking the wrong turn. With relayed shouts along its length, the file was halted. We doubled back on ourselves and waved our final grateful farewells to our lady of the wayside.

As we came within sight of home, my final walking companion was Augustine. Here was curious poetry: he had been first to greet me on my arrival and he was now my final companion on the walk before I set out for home.

Augustine told me he was Dutch and had been twenty

years a Maryknoll Missionary, spending fourteen years as a teacher in the South African townships. 'But more and more I felt a deep pain here,' he rubbed his chest with his fist. 'I somehow knew that I needed to pray as a contemplative.' But how did he discover the Carthusians, I asked once more. His reply was direct and simple: by meditating on the Annunciation, the message contained in Mary's response to the Angel Gabriel. She had said yes promptly to God's word, yet it had taken her a lifetime of prayer to comprehend the meaning in full.

He insisted that only prayer could solve the problems of South African society: and now at last it was beginning to happen. We spoke about the hopeful signs there and of the miracle of the peaceful election. I was able to tell him the story of the first England rugby test when all the touring party had insisted on being on the pitch in order to shake President Mandela's hand. And how having been soundly beaten, Mandela declared, 'We are building a new country, but now we need a rugby team.'

As we came in sight of the monastery, I felt a mix of elation at the deep experience of my stay and sadness at leaving these friends and Christian companions. I knew I would always be close to them in spirit; I felt that not a day would pass without my remembering their day's routine ticking away in prayer and service. I would remember them as individuals, as close friends, above all as a group centred around their charismatic Prior. I would never be one of their number, except in spirit. I hoped it might be possible to return. But even if that were never to happen, I had passed this precious time with them. They had lived their lives openly with me, sharing their routine, treating me as their guest and friend.

I turned to embrace Augustine. We exchanged the kiss of peace, his stubbly beard digging my face. Then too with Bogdan. As we parted, he said softly: 'Please give my regards to your family.' I felt lifted by a more than adequate exchange: a lifelong blessing bestowed for twenty minutes' companionship along the road.

The final words came from Dom Bernard: 'God bless you,

safe journey. And I am sorry I lost my temper.'

The Carthusian confession at the Eucharist prefixes the customary triple list of sins by thought, word and deed with the prior accusation of the sin of pride. I had found little pride at Parkminster.

IN THE CHAPTER HOUSE

Ah! Ah! Ah!.
Richard Methley

IN any account of the English Carthusians, the story of the suppression of the London Charterhouse, the House of the Salutation of the Mother of God, needs to be told, albeit in brief, for no other religious house in Tudor England put up so stout a resistance to Henry VIII's will as he swept away the monasteries in a whirlwind. In all, eighteen Carthusians were done to death before the house was first of all dismembered and finally forced to surrender in November 1538.

In the spring of 1534, the King's matter was growing increasingly urgent. Anne Boleyn's confinement was coming to its term and it was unthinkable that Henry's heir should be born illegitimate; his former marriage to Katherine, that had failed to yield him a son, must be declared null, and his union with the new Queen regularized without further delay. All recourse to Rome had failed; it was time for the King to initiate his own move. The Act of Succession required all subjects called upon to do so to swear an oath that the King's marriage to Anne was valid in God's eyes, since he had never been properly married to Katherine.

The London Charterhouse was the most influential religious house in London. The singular holiness of many of its monks as well as the admirable observance of the community was widely recognized and many came to its cloisters for confession, advice and comfort. In the recent past, several notable university men had entered the community and one in particular, Sebastian Newdigate, had even been a gentleman of the bedchamber to the King.

Sebastian had gone to court as a page and, when still a young man, his youthful good looks and graces, being noticed by the King, had received his seal of approval. His elder sister, Lady Jane Dormer, anxious at her brother's exposure to the Court's worldly ways as the Divorce loomed, took him aside and warned him of following the King's example. His reply shook her: what would you say if you found I had joined the Carthusians? Within a few months, he was as good as his word: her incredulity compelled her to make a personal visit to his superior, Prior Houghton, in order to verify the news.

John Houghton had joined the London Carthusians in the early years of Henry's reign. After reading law at Christ's College, Cambridge, he studied theology privately and was priested some time before entering the House of the Salutation. His talents were soon recognized; he was first sacrist then procurator. In 1530, he was elected prior of Beauvale in Nottinghamshire, but within six months had been recalled to London to be prior there. Under his leadership, the community flourished. His own fervent example and his manner of guiding his community, both young and old, combined to weld them into a formidable house of faithful observance comprising thirty choir monks and eighteen *conversi*. In the ensuing trauma, a protracted and bloody battle of wills that would last more than three years, sixteen of their number were to die.

Within weeks of the Act of Succession, Cromwell's agents were at the Carthusians' gate demanding they take the oath. Prior Houghton's reply was firm: what the King chose to do as regards his marriage was no business of the Carthusians, yet he added that he could see no reason why a marriage that had lasted that long should now of a sudden become void. He was promptly taken with his procurator, Humphrey Middlemore, to the Tower. There Edward Lee, Bishop of York, was to assure them that no element of Faith was at stake, and, agreeing to take the oath, the pair were released back to their community.

The Commissioners followed up this success with a

prompt demand that the entire community should now take the oath. They were met with stubborn refusal. A second and finally a third visitation took place, this time with men-at-arms surrounding the community in their chapter house. At last, they reluctantly followed the footsteps of their prior in recognizing the King's will to marry a new queen to bear him an heir. But this was merely a preamble.

Early the following year, a new measure declared guilty of treason any person who 'denied or refused to acknowledge that the King was Supreme Head of the Church on earth in England'. The Treason Act was to be systematically visited on every religious house in the land. John Houghton, knowing that time was running short, sifted his options. He was protective of his young men (more than half his community were under the age of thirty-five); he thought to swear alone on behalf of them all.

He announced three days of special prayer. On the first, each monk made general confession of all his past sins; on the second, each was reconciled with his brother in respect of all offences they had committed. On the third day, Prior Houghton celebrated a solemn votive Mass of the Holy Spirit. Dom Maurice Chauncy, a monk who in exile was later to chronicle these last days, recorded that at the elevation of the Host 'a gust of wind, an echoing deep harmony, a breath of the Spirit' was felt and heard by all in the church. The prior, who was unable to continue for some moments, later spoke about his experience in chapter, saying that they must all continue to ask God's grace in prayer for steadfast strength.

While they waited, the two priors of Beauvale and Axholme (Norfolk) arrived. Their plan was to forestall the arrival of the Commissioners by asking Cromwell that they might be excused the oath. This was brushed aside. When they maintained resistance, all three priors were taken for examination to the Tower, where Thomas More, Henry's former chancellor, and John Fisher, Bishop of Rochester, were already incarcerated on similar count.

Examined and browbeaten by the Privy Council with no result, they were publicly tried in Westminster Hall in June

1535. Cromwell had to threaten the jury before they would bring in a guilty verdict, and before this he had turned aside several complaints from both judges and the sergeants of the court.

A week later, the three monks were taken from the Tower to be executed at Tyburn. Hanged briefly, they were taken down and butchered into four quarters while still conscious. John Houghton, the first to die, asked the huge crowd that had gathered to witness before the day of judgement that he died rather than deny the teaching of God's church.

His right arm, that had so offended the King, was severed and pinned to the Charterhouse door. He was forty-eight years old.

*

The same day, Thomas Bedyll was sent by Cromwell to confront the rest of the Carthusians. Humphrey Middleton, as vicar, had now taken charge; he was closely supported by William Exmew, his procurator, and Sebastian Newdigate. All three were at once bidden to read a series of anti-papal tracts, but at the end of the day found nothing in them to alter their opinions. The three were removed at once to the Marshalsea, where for the next fortnight they remained chained upright by the legs and neck. It is said that the King visited his former courtier in an effort to persuade him to foreswear. A second trial followed, and this new trio were duly executed on 19th June in the same bloody manner as before.

In this way, the community were deprived of all their officers in less than a month. Cromwell now had the audacity to put in residence two fresh agents. One, John Whalley, taking over the duties of procurator, proceeded to underfeed the monks, complaining that they spent more than their annual income on food alone; while the second, Jasper Fyloll, began a systematic programme of disruption and indoctrination. A series of endless conferences took place, in which the monks were bombarded with arguments aimed at winning their consent. The doors of the house were thrown open to any curious persons who wished to wander through, and several monks were manhandled and assaulted.

Under these circumstances, it became only a matter of time before some members of the community began to weaken and seek to curry favour with their inquisitors. One former monk, Andrew Boorde, although dispensed from his vows, had been living on in the Charterhouse when Cromwell's men arrived. He was freed and sent abroad at the Vicar General's expense, ostensibly to seek a medical school where he could study. In reality, Cromwell was keen to hear from him how the King's actions were being received on the Continent. With some boldness, Boorde made his way to La Grande Chartreuse; on the pretext of confirming his dispensation, he met the Reverend Father. He relayed to him the impression that the London community were making things difficult for the King and stood in need of guidance. Dom Jean Gaillard's response was innocence itself: he charged Boorde to convey his displeasure to the community. He also wrote independently to the Bishop of Lichfield. The brethren must not fail to support the King: was he not named Defender of the Faith by the Pope? He also observed that they seemed to have grown slack in sending obituary notices of their dead. Finally, to ensure future harmonious relations, he told them that he had admitted both the bishop and Cromwell to full confraternity of the Order: in future they should do nothing without consulting him.

The realities in London was otherwise. It was fully two years before Cromwell felt empowered to make any decisive moves. In a preliminary ploy designed to divide and weaken their spirit, he sent four of their leading members – including the future chronicler Maurice Chauncy – to two separate charterhouses in the North. Eight more were sent to spend time with the nuns at Syon, who formerly had supported their cause but had declared in favour of their capitulation.

Then suddenly, the Council made their move: instant suppression unless the oath were taken. The majority gave way (including Chauncy), but ten stood firm – three priests, one deacon and six *conversi*.

The Friday before Whitsun, on 18th May, 1537, the ten monks were taken to Newgate, where they were chained neck and foot. There was to be no trial and no execution. They were denied any food or comfort and left in a foul chamber immobilized together: Bedyll simply observed that they would be 'despeched by thand of God'.

But Mistress Clement, the adopted daughter of Thomas More, was to tend them secretly. By bribing their gaoler and posing as a milkmaid, she was able to bring them food and drink and even some clean linen as they stood without relief. It was soon apparent to the authorities that their lives were being prolonged by some hidden agency, and she was discovered. In spite of being denied access, she still contrived to lower food down to them by removing tiles in the roof. But eventually one by one they died. (A footnote to their deaths is offered by Dom David Knowles in his *The Religious orders in England*, volume III: when Mistress Clement, now over ninety, herself lay dying in exile in Bruges, she kept repeating to her companions that she could not stay much longer since 'the Carthusian fathers stand about my bed and bid me come with them'.) The final victim, Thomas Johnson, expired on 20th September after four months of unimaginable suffering. One of their number, however, had been withdrawn and put on a less cruel regime. He lived on until 1540, when he too suffered the same terrible death at Tyburn. Two other London monks, John Rochester and James Walworth, previously exiled to Hull, had already been hanged in York in 1537.

Henry had had his say. On 15th November, 1538, the London Charterhouse was suppressed, the buildings at once being used to store the King's pavilion and tents.

*

In the chapterhouse at Parkminster, life-size murals placard the martyrs' stand. They are fading now. And it almost seems a mercy: the modern eye finds it hard to linger on such scenes of absolute barbarity depicted 'in all their gory detail', as Dom Cyril commented when taking me round Parkminster at our first encounter. And it is harder still to focus upon the simple black-white issues of those days – King or Pope – when our world of today is a confusion of so many different values, beliefs and conflicting human experience.

Here on the eve of St Bruno's Feast, the Prior gave an exhortation to the community before Vespers. His theme was the complex challenge of renewal set before the Church by the Vatican Council thirty years ago. Dom Cyril's manner is authoritative yet intimate. In his softly spoken Irish he invited both old and young members of the community to take a good, hard look at their predicament. As he spoke, I remembered a Carmelite convent that existed anonymously behind a high brick wall in the heart of North Oxford. Then, of a sudden in the mid-1970s, it was demolished and replaced by upmarket retirement flats. Vocations had simply dried: the nuns had lost their way.

Parkminster has not yet reached that stage, yet the Prior himself described its position as precarious – there are no professed priests, for example, under the age of sixty. And although in recent years recruitment has picked up, perseverance is still poor. Dom Cyril described the experience of a modern novice coming to Parkminster as 'a sort of emigration', so immense are the cultural differences between the contemporary world outside and the lifestyle he is expected to adopt on becoming a Carthusian.

It raises the critical question: can the Carthusian vocation survive without considerable adaptation to contemporary culture? The immediate response, especially from the older Carthusians, is likely to be emphatic. And they would point to their 900 years of unchanging fidelity to Bruno's legacy. Yet already since the Council considerable changes have been accepted, both in devolving regulation from the centre to individual houses and more especially to admitting the brothers as fully integrated community members with the choir monks.

Dom Cyril is open to the future and foresees more changes still to come; but he firmly believes that the contemplative life initiated by the charisma of St Bruno corresponds to a deep human need and experience, so that it will always be an integral part of Christ's Church.

At the end of his address, Dom Cyril prostrated, lying sideways in the endearing Carthusian way, as if victim to some sudden accident. It was the anniversary of his own profession and he was asking for his brothers' prayers.

*

Dom Cyril's address brings to an end this account of the Carthusians living and praying in England today as the millennium approaches. Given my subject, there have perhaps been too many words. They took some tracking down, these shy Carthusians. I still rejoice at my encounter, for here I found a secret pulsing heart of love, observance and faith. Simon – who read the book of nature – warned me that my book would be hard to write, since I could never enter the cell. And he was right.

But there was one Carthusian long ago who spoke of his daily experience in a journal that he kept. Richard Furth was born outside Leeds in 1451 at a village named Methley, a name he took. It was only a few miles from the birthplace of another English mystic, Richard Rolle.

At the age of twenty-five, Richard Methley joined the Carthusians at Mount Grace in Yorkshire. He always ascribed his vocation to having given alms to an aged, paralyzed ancress a few days before her death. For within three months, he had joined the Order.

He wrote a number of works on the spiritual life and we have a transcription of *The Cloud of Unknowing* in his own hand. (The English Carthusians were diligent copyists of manuscripts and in particular gave their skills to the works of the English mystics. As a sole result of their labours we have surviving texts of *The Cloud*, as well as the writings of Margery Kempe. It is certain in my mind that Julian of Norwich comes to us through the London charterhouse of Sheen.)

But Richard Methley's most endearing work is a brief personal diary running from the Feast of Bruno, 6th October, 1487, until 15th December following. In it comes a passage worth quoting in full, since it offers a rare and open insight into the commonplace mystical experience of the Carthusian monk then and since:

Ineffable is the yearning of love. But if naught were said of it haply some might say that it was a thing of naught; and so, following God's will, I will set out as best I can what I have experienced. And if I cannot tell it as it is, yet I do not doubt that what I am about to say is true. Since, then, one who has had experience bids thanksgiving be made to God, he who has not experienced it should not impugn it out of envy for the solitary.

On the feast of St Peter in Chains [1st August] I was in the church at Mount Grace, and after celebrating Mass was engaged upon thanksgiving in prayer and meditation, when God visited me in power, and I yearned with love so as almost to give up the ghost. How this could be I will tell you, my brethren, as best I can by the grace of God. Love and longing for the Beloved raised me in spirit into heaven, so that save for this mortal life nothing (so far as I know) would have been lacking to me of the glory of God Who sitteth on the throne. Then did I forget all pain and fear and deliberate thought of anything, and even of the Creator. And as men who fear the peril of fire do not cry 'Fire hath come upon my house; come ye and help me', since in their strait and agony they can scarce speak a single word, but cry 'Fire, Fire, Fire!' or, if their fear be greater they cry 'Ah! Ah! Ah!', wishing to impart their peril in this single cry, so I, in my poor way. For first I oft commended my soul to God, saying: 'Into thy hands,' either in words or (as I think rather) in spirit. But as the pain of love grew more powerful I could scarce have thought at all, forming within my spirit these words: 'Love! Love! Love!' And at last, ceasing from this, I deemed that I would wholly yield up my soul, singing, rather than crying, in spirit through joy. 'Ah! Ah! Ah!'

He is praying before the stone statue of Our Lady above the little altar in his oratory. He feels the wind upon his cheek blowing through the new, unfinished window he has asked to be made to let in more light and air. Each morning as he rises, he puts on his habit, thanking God for his vocation and aware of how many men depended upon Carthusian prayers for their own salvation and that of those dear to them.

Secretum meum mihi, 'My secrets are my own', was the watchword of those both before and after. At least we can be grateful to Richard Methley that this once he gave us some glimpse of the hidden Carthusian life.

"This book is begun by God's gift and his grace:
but it is not yet performed, as I see it."

Julian of Norwich

MOST BOOKS must be closed – with perhaps a sigh of regret – as they end. And that is that. But this particular book has come alive again: Hear our Silence is now an open invitation for all to encounter the Carthusian tradition of prayer, what we call the Prayer of Silence. And it happened this way.

Having met them once, these Carthusians would not go away. Or rather I made up my own reasons for creeping back. I needed a little more research, I explained to the Prior, just to put the final touches to my book. And I returned for another week, this time in the depths of winter. Tough men those Carthusians, creeping along the cloister to church for Matins when the temperature in February has dropped well below zero. But the book was finally complete and sent to my publisher. So that was that.

But the memories were still vivid, the Carthusian model of Silent Prayer somehow engrained in the psyche. Presently, my wife and I began to pray together in silence for half an hour each day. We told a friend, asked her if she would like to join us. "Well, I'd have to come and try it, "she replied. She came, tasted the Silence and came again. Others too joined in as each Thursday at 6.30 our door was ajar, inviting anyone to the Prayer of Silence.

Came the day that I went back to Parkminster and told Dom Cyril that I would like to take their silence and offer it around to people outside.

"Use our name," he said, with a generosity that took my breath away.

And so we carefully forged our plans. We looked long and hard at what we began to call "the model". How we shaped the framework of our Half Hour Silence. One may think this over scrupulous, why deliberate on something so simple. But the shape is important, each detail counts.

Finally this became our model:

The model takes its name and inspiration from the silence of

Carthusian prayer, the seeker who journeys into the silent desert of the heart to encounter God.

The invitation is simply to half an hour of silent prayer and is open to all – all faiths, all conditions, all are welcome.

The setting is a peaceful room, a waiting circle around a lighted candle, quietening music or chant. Five or so minutes after the group has come together, there is a short reading. This is done by the group leader, slowly and prayerfully, and leads into the silence.

What each person does with this silence is his or her own personal experience– sharing the silence, the journey in common.

The silence is slowly dissolved after half an hour by the return of the music; when the group is ready, a sign of peace is offered and received... followed by dispersal.

(No tea and biscuits, no chat – the Silence is precious and each takes it away within themselves.)

Next we decided on a public launch at Sarum College, Salisbury. We wrote to all our friends and contacts; and over fifty people supported the day long event. As the time drew closer, I wrote to Dom Cyril asking for the community's prayers and wondering if he would be kind enough to offer us an inclusive invitation to prayer.

There is always a fairly long silence when you write to a Carthusian, that is their way. But presently the post arrived from Parkminster. On the reverse side of the envelope I had addressed to the Prior came 221 close-write words. This was far more than I had anticipated – no mere invitation, this amounted to our Charter. We hold it dear to this day:

Prayer + Love

Asking people to pray is like telling the wind to blow,
the ear to listen, the eye to see.
We cannot not pray, anymore than not be, once given the gift of existence.
We can only shut it out or deny it.

Prayer is simply the conscious dimension of being
when it opens out to receive all that it is:
gift, marvellously, gratuitously there;
word of communion with all things,
who hears their silence of wonder,
adoration before Him who is
the source and end of all.

Prayer is also the birthing of the person,
the creative revelation each is called to become,
the etching of a mysterious face
reflected by the Mystery we contemplate,
the knowing of God
as we come to know ourselves,
Spirit breathed
by the Thou who calls and loves.

Silence then is the plenitude of the Word.

Once in France, a Zen priest, a recognized master, came to our monastery asking to be taught how to pray, pray to the Other that is, for he could distinguish between meditation and prayer, symbiosis and dialogue. We talked of our different conceptions of things and measured the distance that separated us. We prayed in silence, side by side, over several months and experienced the communion that united us.

Prayer ultimately is love.

That communion I wish you all. † Cyril
Peace and Joy in Christ St Hugh's Charterhouse February 20 1999
© *Hear our Silence*

As WELL as this public event, we launched our very own website. My son, Charles, is an expert programmer and so we were gifted by his skills. One of his first suggestions, was for our logo: why not have a hovering kestrel, the windhover, as Hopkins names the bird in his poem dedicated "to Christ our Lord".

We call our invitation *Hear our Silence*, the logical outcome of this book, adding a descriptive, "people at prayer", rather in the manner of those road signs which read "men at work".

We began to offer workshops. Single days or across the weekend, when people could come together to experience the Prayer of Silence and share by exploring as a group the nature of prayer and why it is special for themselves. And resulting from these workshop explorations, house groups began to spring up along the same lines as our Thursday evening half hour of Silent Prayer.

But progress, inevitably, was slow. I remember a wise lady friend of my wife saying at our launch day, "this will work, but it will take time." By nature an impulsive maverick, I did not fancy this saying. I was all for off--right now.

Yet we had to learn patience. The simple lesson that the Lord's time is in *his* own good time. We may not manufacture the moment. And then, suddenly, his time did come.

"Why not write about it in *Saga*," said my wife one day. So I picked up the phone to the features editor and realized that Edna Tromans was listening to what I was telling her – about the Prayer of Silence and these mysterious Carthusian monks. I said I thought we might be given access to Parkminster for some discreet photographs, as an alluring visual background to my story.

I wrote my piece and the Prior agreed to a photo session. *Saga's* talented new Art Director, Chris White, confessed to living in Henfield, the very same village by Parkminster. Not surprisingly, he was keen as the hare to view its hidden secrets. He told me that he had a very special photographer in mind for the task, Graham Harrison who had worked for a long stint on *The Telegraph Magazine*. To my astonishment, he hails from Thame where my wife and I had started The Red House Bookshop, our children's bookselling business, now long since handed on to others.

The article appeared in July, 2000. It was the longest *Saga* piece in living memory. The layout was blissfully generous, Graham's pics stunning. I knew at once that we were in for a total blitz of readers' letters. And sure enough they came – by the hundred. At last, we had water under our keel.

Thanks to *Saga Magazine's* bold initiative in taking prayer for real, *Hear our Silence* now has a growing audience. "Be still, and know in the Silence that I am your Lord", the words of the Psalmist ring in my ears. His the timing, his the initiative, for it is his work, not mine.

I will end this book with four readings, a spread of our weekly texts with which we introduce the Silent half hour of Prayer. They dwell on the nature of that encounter with the Other, our Maker, Father, Mother – our Again-Maker, as Julian calls Christ.

Let them speak for themselves in your innermost heart, inviting you "to dwell there in peace", the peace of his Abiding Presence.

Hear our Silence
People at Prayer

making a start

Prayer of its very nature is always a beginning
our best approach it is that of a beginner

Each time we pray
we witness creation
in the freshness of the first morning

Each time we enter into our soul
in quiet presence
we are created from within
by a life-giving surge of Being

As a child we receive and discover in wonder
This is why we never tire of prayer
why it is always new

you cannot repeat prayer
you can only receive each new moment
in it's utter newness
each new prayer

We do not "know" how to pray,
but there is a spirit within who does

Cyril

Hear our Silence
People at Prayer

beyond self

In the silence of self
I encounter an Other
far greater than the I of me

As the seed pushes roots into soil
as its leaves reach out to sunlight
the self cannot help but expand
into the ground of the Other
discovering new life
opening ourselves to Living Love
(JS)

Hear our Silence
People at Prayer

attending to God

Attentiveness to the deepest self
leads one beyond self

Prayer is entering into the depths of the heart
and dwelling there in peace

listening that is receptive
responsive to this mystery of faith

Attentiveness to God
is the work
of faith and love
its fruit is the union
of love and knowledge
to which it gives birth

Attentiveness to self
attentiveness to God
are like two interdepedent
complementary movements--
the breathing of our deepest being

The Way of Silent Love, conf. XIII, by a Carthusian

Hear our Silence
People at Prayer

Late have I loved you

So late have I loved you
Beauty ancient
yet so new

I have come to love you now
yet so late in the day

You were within me
but I was in the world outside myself
I sought you outside myself
wantonly misguided
I wallowed in the beauty
of those creatures you had made

You were Still within me
but I was not with you

The very beauty of the world
kept me far from you
and yet unless each one of them
had all not been in you
they could have had no being

You called out to me
you cried my name
at last you burst through my deafness

You flashed forth
upon me
your light surrounded me
I was blind no more

I tasted
now I hunger
and thirst for you

Your finger touches me
I surrender to your loving peace

Saint Augustine, The Confessions